DUMB
CAREER

TOP TEN DUMB CAREER MISTAKES
...and how to avoid them

LONA O'CONNOR

VGM Career Horizons
NTC/Contemporary Publishing Group

Library of Congress Cataloging-in-Publication Data

O'Connor, Lona.
    Top ten dumb career mistakes . . . and how to avoid them / Lona O'Connor.
      p.   cm.
    ISBN 0-8442-6313-3
    1. Vocational guidance.   2. Career development.   I. Title.
    HF5381.0453   1998   98-8344
    650.1—dc21   CIP

Cover design by Scott Rattray
Interior design by Nancy J. Howard/NK Graphics

Published by VGM Career Horizons
A division of NTC/Contemporary Publishing Group, Inc.
4255 West Touhy Avenue, Lincolnwood (Chicago), Illinois 60646-1975 U.S.A.
Copyright © 1999 by NTC/Contemporary Publishing Group, Inc.
All rights reserved. No part of this book may be reproduced, stored in a retrieval system, or
transmitted in any form or by any means, electronic, mechanical, photocopying, recording, or
otherwise, without the prior permission of NTC/Contemporary Publishing Group, Inc.
Printed in the United States of America
International Standard Book Number: 0-8442-6313-3

18 17 16 15 14 13 12 11 10 9 8 7 6 5 4 3 2 1

This book is dedicated to my family, who gave me the love and courage to learn from my own mistakes; and to those longtime readers of my newspaper column who kept asking, "When are you going to write a book?"

Contents

Introduction

How This Book Came About

Over the 15 years I've been writing a career advice col-
umn, I began to notice certain patterns in the questions I got
from readers. They were getting chewed up by office politics, by
burnout, by stagnation, by fighting with people instead of making
allies out of them. I could see them sabotaging themselves over
and over again in the same ways. Different people, same mistakes.
Not dumb people, but dumb mistakes. And for what it's worth,
I've made most of those same mistakes myself (and a few others
too). But that's another book.

There is hope: most of the dumb career mistakes we make are
avoidable. And even if you've already made the mistake, you can
usually dig yourself out of it. You don't need any charts or graphs

or complicated strategies to get back on course. In most cases, you can solve a career problem by being honest with yourself and others, by being direct, and by maintaining your values.

How to Use This Book

If you're the sort of person who reads a book from start to finish, that's great. You're an author's best friend. But if you're like me, you're probably going to want to jump around in the book, starting with the career mistake that's bothering you right now. That's fine too. Each chapter is designed to help you work on a particular problem. Mistake by mistake—and solution by solution—here's what you will find in each chapter.

1. *Getting Off to a Bad Start.* In this chapter, you will find many of the classic mistakes people make when starting out with a new job, new company, new department, or new boss: falling in with a "bad" crowd, not learning the corporate culture, ticking off the wrong people. If you want more information on setting yourself up well, read the chapter on office politics (Chapter 6).
2. *Alienating Your Boss.* If you seem to have a lot of problems with your boss, this is the chapter for you. Consider reading it more than once. It will show you how to neutralize the worst of bosses and turn some of them into your best ally.
3. *Having a Bad Attitude.* If your problems at work are always somebody else's fault, if there is always some reason why you fail, you need an attitude adjustment.
4. *Not Having Goals.* It's easy to drift in a job. One day you're 25; the next you're 55, and you still haven't gotten off the dime. This chapter helps you define your goals. It also reminds you of the importance of goals in motivating you and keeping you focused. And it gives you step-by-step methods to accomplish your goals.

5. *Mishandling Conflict.* Most of the exchanges between you and your co-workers involve some sort of conflict. In this chapter, you will learn how to redefine conflict as negotiation. You will also learn about how to channel your anger into getting what you want.

6. *Misplaying Office Politics.* Office politics has gotten a bad reputation. It has been defined as conniving, scheming, and cheating your way to the top—*tricks.* This chapter is a no-tricks guide to office politics. It allows you to steer your way through misinformation, gossip, and rivalries, getting what you want in a way that doesn't compromise your values.

7. *Suffering from a Rotten Image.* In its most recognizable form, this is called *secretary syndrome*—getting typecast in a low-level job no matter how talented and ambitious you are. It can also show up in ways that are mysterious to you: you think you're doing a good job, but no one takes you seriously. This chapter includes an image makeover.

8. *Succumbing to Stress and Burnout.* It happens to the best of us. Even if you love your job, there's bound to be a morning when you wake up and just don't want to do it anymore. This chapter also discusses the most vicious form of burnout, which results from trying to "have it all."

9. *Stagnating.* When your job becomes a no-brainer, you've become stagnant. You're not growing in your job anymore; you're doing the same tasks over and over. This chapter offers suggestions on how to get out of your rut and discusses how to use your job plateau to get your perspective back.

10. *Letting Go of Your Dreams.* The biggest career mistake you can make is to have a dream and let it go—or, worse, not even to allow yourself to have a dream. Dreams are related to goals, but they are bigger and usually closer to your heart of hearts. They take longer to accomplish than regular goals, and they are usually more risky. But they can take you places you never dreamed you could go.

Chapter 1

Getting Off
to a Bad Start

What Am I Doing Here?

You're starting a new job. You can either get off on the right foot or stick your foot in your mouth. How do you make yourself a part of this new work culture?

Your first responsibility is to do your job well. Other things are important, but nothing is as important as that. Don't make the mistake of thinking you're supposed to understand everything after one brief orientation. It takes time. Get clear instructions from your supervisor. During the first few days and weeks, while you're still in learning mode, ask questions when you don't understand.

Good Impressions

It's natural to want to make a good impression on all your new co-workers and to worry that people won't like you. Don't wait for your co-workers to come to you; introduce yourself to everyone you meet. People are always curious about new workers in a company, so satisfy their need to know. Be sure to offer each person basic information about yourself: who you are, where you work, and what you do.

If you have time, you can continue the conversation with a question or other conversation starter: "Hi, I'm Mary Farmer. I'm new in the claims processing department and I'm here to pick up the Welch Corporation file. I worked at Consolidated before I came here. Jack Trilling said to say hi to you." If possible, ask the new co-workers you meet to tell you about themselves and their jobs. Listen well as they tell you. No matter how overwhelmed you are by all the new sensations and unknown faces, make an effort to get to know people. It's just as important to orient yourself to your co-workers as to your duties. During this "glad to meet you" period, you can be gathering valuable information about how things get done and who's who.

You are projecting that all-important first impression of yourself, which will stick with people for a long time—so present yourself in the most positive light. If you were to hang back, for example, word could spread around the office that you are stuck-up. So you might as well control the image people are forming.

Getting the News

Here comes an important rule of the workplace. Memorize it. There are two main types of truth in an office culture: the official version and what really goes on. The official version is interesting mainly as something against which you can compare what really goes on—who's really in power, title or not; who's in bed with whom, literally or professionally.

If you get invited to any after-work gatherings of your co-workers, you'll find out quickly the second type of truth. As you did in the office, talk about yourself enough to answer people's questions and quench their curiosity, and then sit back and listen—and learn.

And please, don't drink too much. There's a tendency to do so when you're ill at ease with new people. If you get bombed, blab about your salary or your marital problems, dance on a table, or do anything else foolish, you'll fit in all right—you'll immediately become the new office buffoon.

Another good source of unofficial information about your workplace is secretaries and executive assistants. The best ones zip their lips, but if you build a good relationship with them (and they *will* know if you're just using them), they can pass along useful information. Like when the Big Guy is in his office and whether he might have time to talk with you—or when he's in a foul mood and it would be better just to stay out of his way.

As you develop your sources of information, in all cases take what you hear with a grain of salt. Wait and observe. Then draw your own conclusions based on all the evidence, including your own observations.

Striking Out

No matter how hard you try, some people are bound to seem standoffish to you. In the first place, it's just not statistically possible that everyone will like you. In the second place, if you're new at this place of work, you don't know exactly where you have stepped in that murky pond called office politics. The person who does not seem to warm up to you may have wanted the job you got or may be a loyal friend of the person who wanted the job but didn't land it. Of course, it's impossible for you to know this right away. As time passes, you will learn the local brand of office politics as well as individual personalities. Your job, now and in the future, is to remain neutral and friendly to all your co-workers.

The Wrong Clique

Worse than having certain people dislike you is to fall in too soon with the wrong clique. Notice who spends time with whom; who spends a lot of time in the boss's office; who has a lot of people dropping by his desk. Information like this will help you distinguish the cliques, the good, the bad, the leaders, the followers, the troublemakers.

One safe strategy is not to ally yourself too closely with anyone soon after starting a job. That way you don't risk alienating people who might have been your allies—and you don't have the problem of extracting yourself from a group later, when you realize it's not the one for you.

Another strategy is to ask different people out to lunch during your first weeks on the job. Avoid the tendency to blather on about yourself, and just listen and observe. Let them tell you about the office. While they are doing so, you can observe how they reveal themselves—happy or malcontent, poorly treated or on the rise.

The ones you want to avoid are those who communicate a negative attitude about everything and everybody. Hook up with people like that and you might as well strap concrete boots onto your career. You're looking for people who are upbeat, energetic, and on the move. After all, that is the kind of worker you are, isn't it?

Harnessing Chaos: Getting Control of a New Job

Let's assume you're able to avoid some of the social and political pitfalls of entering a new corporate culture. You also have to be able to do the job well, even if you've never done it before.

Starting a new job is like trying to harness chaos. You probably possess most of the skills you need—why else would you have gotten this job? But now you have to exercise them all at once, maybe for the first time. Oh, the pressure! You may soon begin to wish you had stuck with your old familiar job.

One of the most vexing aspects of a new job is that you often don't know how long things will take. And naturally you're going to be slower to complete new tasks because you have to think your way through every operation. That's why learning to do something can be so much harder than just doing it.

Bottom line, you can get hopelessly behind in a very short time. You may even suffer the world's fastest case of burnout if anxiety, perfectionism, and fatigue get to you before you master the job. But you can survive the first few weeks on a new job if you strive to pace yourself well and keep your perspective.

Managing Time

To keep your new job from overwhelming you, you need to practice some important principles of organization and time management.

You can organize your time more effectively if you find out first how long the task normally takes. This is one of the questions you should ask the person who is training you or an experienced co-worker. For the first few times you work on something new, allow yourself about double the normal time.

Of course, each time you do a task, you should stay conscious of the passing time and aim for that ideal deadline. As you evaluate how you're doing, improving your speed is one of the goals you must meet. However, by building in "screw-up time," you're less likely to get quite so frustrated and upset during the learning process.

Inevitably, this also can mean that you'll be working longer hours, especially at first. If you think you can avoid this, you're wrong. By trying to get a new job done in the time it takes to do a job you know, you're actually putting unnecessary pressure on yourself. For now, live with the extra hours, knowing that they won't last forever, and neither will this start-up stress.

Ask Questions

If the person who preceded you in the job is not available to answer your questions, be sure to identify someone else (perhaps several people) who can supply at least partial answers about how things work.

Find out: When are things due? Who can help you if something goes wrong? Which tasks can be done in advance? Who can help? Take notes as you're learning, and remember: even if you get a thorough briefing, there will be plenty of details nobody told you about.

Stuff Happens

Expect things to go wrong. You don't yet know what are the normal snafus of this new job—and of course, if they had told you before you started, you'd probably have run away screaming. But if you assume that things will go wrong, at least you won't be paralyzed by shock when they do.

Ask for Help

If you get stuck, don't quietly sink into the mud. Tell somebody you need help. At this early stage, it's not only unnecessary, but dangerous to struggle too long with a problem. Speak up: you will be able to solve the immediate problem, and you'll also avoid the self-destructive and stress-inducing tendency to criticize yourself for not knowing.

Stressed for Success

At the end of the day, you'll probably say, "I'm so exhausted, but I didn't really get that much *done!*" The effort of thinking your way through every aspect of your work; dealing with unfamiliar problems and new people; and working longer hours *is* exhausting, so cut yourself some slack.

Cool It

During your learning period, don't take on any responsibilities you can avoid. You may start out energetic and optimistic, as if you can do anything. Resist giving in to that feeling, because it will lure you to overcommit yourself. Stick to the job at hand for at least a month, or three months, or however long it takes until you know it by heart.

Don't expect too much of yourself right now; as much as possible, put aside any perfectionist tendencies. Expect to make mistakes and to forget things; rely on lists and double-check your work. Ask for help.

Nothing Is Forever

Especially if you're feeling discouraged, memorize one of the great rules of work: There is always a time lag between effort and payoff. So if you hang in there and don't panic, all that extra effort you put into the learning process will start to accumulate. One day you'll walk into your office and realize that it's starting to get easier. The realization will just hit you: "I know how to do this!" Enjoy that pleasant sensation. You earned it.

Remember Why You're Doing It

Whatever the reasons you took this job, recite them to yourself at least once a day. Money, advancement, benefits—whatever your reasons, they can sustain you through rough times and help you keep plugging away.

But I've Never Done This Before! (How to Handle a New Assignment)

There are some things about any job that nobody can teach you. Let's say you proposed a new project, or suppose you were hired to start a new department. It's all yours to create. Now, where do you start?

Starting any new job is hard enough, but this is different. Your responsibility now is to create something from the ground up, something you've never done before, maybe something that didn't exist before. If you don't get a grip—and fast—you could fail or, worse, do a mediocre job.

Whenever you're starting something new, it's important to remember that about 80 percent of your efforts will go into the start-up. And they should, because the better you set up any new endeavor, the more smoothly it will end up working on a day-to-day basis.

The Devil You Know

One of the most intimidating things about a new task is its unknown nature. You need to translate a vague mission statement into a list of small, familiar tasks. So instead of lying sleepless in the dark worrying about it, keep a notepad with you at all times and jot down what needs to be done, when, and by whom. To calm your inevitable anxiety and solve problems at the same time, keep asking yourself, "How is this like something else that I've done before?" When you can identify a task as being like something familiar, you simplify the task. And don't limit your thinking to work procedures alone. You may master a new task by realizing that it's like baking cookies or changing the oil in your car.

Don't Flail About

Sometimes when starting a new project, you will have the impulse to try every possible solution, every variation on a theme, in the panicky hope that one of them will be right. There is no harm in writing such possibilities down and discussing them with your team. However, part of the start-up process should be to evaluate such ideas in terms of how much benefit you might get in return for the effort. Remember: you don't have the resources to do everything. Working smart means picking the tasks that appear to give the greatest results from your limited resources.

Problems, Problems

It's easy to slip into a negative frame of mind, particularly when problems start cropping up. To guard against defeatism, make a list of expected problems. For every problem you list, write at least one solution. This lures your mind away from fear and into positive thinking and problem solving.

Establish Patterns

The mind loves structure. It functions better and gets less anxious when it can build a structure in which to operate. So from the beginning of your project, make it a habit to look for patterns that will help you give a structure to the project.

Patterns include times of day when things need to be done, when people can be reached, and when bottlenecks occur. Recognizing and working with such patterns will help you begin to control your work immediately, and this experience will serve you the next time you start a new task.

Another way to use patterns to help you control the task is to arrange tasks in groups. This will increase your efficiency, concentration, accuracy, and control. Group similar tasks together (letter writing, phone calls, appointments) and then do them in blocks of an hour or two at a time.

Never underestimate the power of orderly procedures. Just as surgeons and artists lay out their tools the same way each time and pilots run through their checklists before taking off, you can and should establish checklists and methods. These strategies save energy, keeping you from having to re-invent your work procedure each time. They also help you to avoid making mistakes and forgetting things.

Once Is Not Enough

Arranging an unknown task into known patterns is something you should continue to do throughout the start-up process of your new project. Because the project is in a constant state of change, things that worked yesterday may need adjusting today. Another rule to memorize, for now and for later: Don't expect things to stay exactly the same.

When Do You Need It Done?

One of the greatest sources of stress in a new endeavor is the feeling that you cannot possibly finish all the work on time. By naming and grouping tasks, you have solved the first part of this puzzle. You can further overcome this fear and assure that you will finish the job on time by establishing subdeadlines. Say, for instance, that you have a firm start-up date and you have already grouped your tasks. Now arrange those groups of tasks in order of priority and assign deadlines for completing them.

Bad Control, Good Control

It's a mistake to think that you must control every act of the people working with you. That's bad control, which will make both you and them crazy in no time. A better form of control (and a better use of your time) is to keep making sure that people are working toward the ultimate goal of your project. Your main task is to plan the strategy for how that will happen.

Share the Load

This is your project, of course, but you will be making a big mistake if you do not share responsibility. If you are working with others, you should delegate tasks (and deadlines) to them. Besides easing your workload and worry, delegating serves the important function of enlarging the pool of people with ideas and solutions. Don't be too proud to seek advice from experienced co-workers. If you pick those who have helpful attitudes, you can get insights that will save you time and frustration.

The Frustrations of That First Job

Dear Lona,

I am a recent graduate of the University of Michigan. Although I have a BA in communications, I have no interest in the communications field. I was able to get an internship in human resources for a small company. I enjoy the work and I now want to pursue a career in human resources.

Here is my problem: I am learning nothing about human resources, but I'm acquiring plenty of secretarial skills! I have learned various computer programs, but I still don't feel challenged.

I am now ready to look for a permanent position in personnel, but I'm afraid I will still appear inexperienced. I'm starting to feel depressed because I know of classmates who are making $20,000 to $30,000, and they have no more work experience than I do.

1. Did I waste my time with this internship?
2. Why do employers want so much work experience for entry-level positions?
3. Am I underemploying myself?

Dear Intern,

1. You haven't wasted your time if you have learned something (even those computer skills) that you can add to your resume. Even more valuable, you have learned what you really want to do. There are some people who never figure that out.

2. Employers can demand a lot of work experience for entry-level jobs when there are more applicants than there are available jobs. The cost of training and developing workers is high, so employers want to get the best for their money. Face it: lack of experience is a common problem on the first couple of jobs you have after you leave school. Fortunately, you have solved part of that problem and gotten some experience by getting at least your toe in the door with a human resources job. Even if you haven't learned as much as you had hoped, you have at least earned the first relevant credit for your resume.

3. At this moment, yes, you probably are underemployed. But you can make plans to change that immediately. Even though you are planning to leave this job, make sure you have exhausted its possibilities. Tell your boss you want to learn more skills.

Pinpoint a problem at the office that you can solve. Think up a useful project or volunteer to help your boss with the real work of your department. If your boss gives you the go-ahead, you will not be wasting any more of your time, and you won't be bored.

But please don't announce to your boss that you're planning to leave! Your morale will be far better if you have one job while you are searching for the next one. It will also help if you brace yourself for a long job search.

Getting the Next Job

You may well seem inexperienced to those who interview you during the next few weeks. Your best resource at this point in your career is your eagerness to learn. Emphasize that in interviews. Give specific examples of responsibilities you have taken on.

Now that you've settled on a career direction, you can focus your job search. If there are no job openings, request some informational interviews with decision makers in local companies. They can help you develop valuable contacts that eventually can lead to opportunities.

Read trade journals so you'll be knowledgeable about issues in your field. The journals may also provide job leads and names of people with whom you can interview. Join the local chapter of your professional association and start hunting for a mentor.

No Self-Torture Allowed

Try not to compare yourself with your classmates who seem to be racing ahead of you in salary or status. This is a particularly cruel form of self-torture, because there is always someone who seems to be doing better than you. Concentrate instead on getting the best position according to your standards, not someone else's. There's nothing wrong with wanting more money, and there's nothing wrong with a little well-channeled envy—as long as those emotions motivate you without becoming your obsession.

Too Much Responsibility

Dear Lona,
　　You got me in a lot of trouble. I followed your advice and talked my boss into giving me more responsibilities. Now I

think I might have taken on more than I can handle. What should I do?

Dear Reader,

Give yourself time to flounder in this new situation. If you had told me that you slipped right into this extra responsibility and had it completely under control in a month, I would be concerned that you had taken too easy a job. Trading one unchallenging job for another is a waste of time and energy.

Unpleasant as it may feel, it is actually a more promising sign if you feel out of your depth. Frequently, ambitious people can talk their way into jobs that are too tough for them. And we can forget how frustrating the learning process can be. If you stick with it, the process of growing into that bigger job ultimately will sharpen your abilities.

It is natural to feel anxious. You have deliberately taken yourself out of a safe routine and volunteered for something unknown and difficult. Your nervousness is akin to the stagefright that actors experience before performances.

Make Stagefright Work for You

Stagefright can keep you sharp. Because you are unsure of yourself, you will double-check your work, you will ask a lot more questions, and you will work harder to get everything just right.

Keep your perspective. When you're working late and feeling sorry for yourself, remember the good reasons why you asked for this job. Maybe it positions you for the job you really want, and you know you can use the extra money for a real vacation. Reminding yourself of long-term goals and benefits makes the daily drudgery easier to survive.

There is a remote chance that this job is actually more than you can handle; that's why they invented three-month evaluations. Give yourself three months of maximum effort to get on top of things. If you are still experiencing problems, discuss them with your boss and be ready to suggest solutions.

Because you are experiencing a lapse in self-confidence, you probably have forgotten a very important point: Your boss thinks you can handle this job and wants you to succeed. Otherwise, she would not have offered you this chance. Smart bosses don't like disruptions in work flow and they don't like failures, which reflect badly on their managing abilities. So they pick people they think can master the job. They know that people who volunteer are usually more committed to succeed. So borrow your boss's confidence in you, and yours will return soon enough.

I Hate My New Job!

Dear Lona,

I have been working for a month at a new job, and I hate it. All my friends told me this was a great opportunity that would make my future. Now I think maybe they were wrong. I was really looking forward to it, and now I think maybe I made a mistake. Should I just quit and get this over with?

Dear Reader,

You are not allowed to quit until you have analyzed why you are unhappy and have done what you can to improve the job you have. The letdown you describe is very predictable. A number of factors may be conspiring to make you question your decision to take this job.

Put on the brakes for a minute and answer some questions. What parts of the job do you dislike? Is it the hours, the pace, your co-workers? Are you disillusioned because you had an exaggerated or inaccurate idea of what the job would be like? Were you so excited that you set yourself up for a disappointment?

Once you have broken down your complaints into components, ask yourself what you can change right now. If you are working a late shift and it is ruining your family life, ask your boss if your schedule can be altered. Just because you are the new kid doesn't mean you shouldn't tell your boss about your legitimate concerns. Make it worth your boss's while by pointing out ways you can be more useful on a different shift.

Many jobs are unpleasant in themselves but are valuable stepping stones to the more attractive jobs that come after you have paid your dues. If you are currently in such a job, you would be wise to hang on a few months longer. Give yourself a goal of moving up to the next stage in the minimum amount of time it will take. During this period, everything you do should be aimed at winning the promotion or gaining the experience to move on. You also would be wise to remind the boss of your goals.

Even if you eventually decide you have made a mistake, one month isn't really very much time to evaluate a job. Your company probably gave itself at least three months of probation. You should do the same, continuing to watch closely for other opportunities.

Remember that you are experiencing the old problem of expectations versus reality. Part of you wants any new situation to solve all your problems; it's a natural hope. But the part of you that keeps you going is the realist who says, "No, it's not working out perfectly, but it's definitely an improvement. And I'm taking steps to make it better." So don't jump to premature conclusions. Give yourself time to succeed.

Should You Quit?

Before you quit a job you dislike, analyze. Rethink your decision. Carefully go back over the reasons you took this new job. You weighed the job you were leaving against the job you took. You compared salary, opportunities, working conditions, benefits. Such decisions are seldom black-and-white. Undoubtedly you had to give up some things to gain others.

Which of your original doubts are resurfacing? Are you, for instance, wondering if your larger salary is worth the extra hours you're now working? It is vital that you honestly answer these questions, relying on your personal values about work.

What Do You Value?

Originally, you may have been attracted by the money. (Aren't we all?) Now you have come to realize how important free time is to you. This is one of the great ironies of life: as soon as you achieve one thing, you learn the value of something else.

So now is a good time to remind yourself of your long-term goals and values and how your new job can fulfill them. If the increased salary will make it possible for you to buy a home or provide better daycare for your children, you may decide that the extra hours are worth it.

If, on the other hand, you are losing touch with your family, you may have to make adjustments. For example, you may be able to shift your hours so that you can spend more time with your family.

Did you let yourself get sweet-talked into this job? Did you understand fully the reasons why your new company wanted you? Were those reasons compatible with your own reasons for accepting the job? Often, your goals and your company's goals may be different—and if you're like most people, you probably did not even raise such concerns during the interview process, which has some of the same self-delusions as dating. The job itself, like marriage, can be a real wake-up call.

Look Back

Rethink the reasons you left your old job. If you decided it was a dead end, do you still feel this is true? Could you really go back to that job? And, if it comes to that, how easily could you find yet another job? These are all very sobering questions, but they can help you zero in on specific problems instead of vague anxieties. If you find yourself more confused now, table the discussion and take a breather. Go for a walk; see a movie. Resume your thinking when you feel refreshed.

Risk Plus Change

Consider other factors that may be shaking your confidence. If taking a risk is difficult for you, as it is for most people, you may be anxious just because a new job is a risk.

Changing jobs, even for the better, is guaranteed to cause stress. Think about your first day of work. You were introduced to dozens of people and were desperately trying to remember their names and which of them (all of them!) you were supposed to impress. You entered a new system of office politics, trying to figure out who is who and who's already jealous of you just because you're the new kid (or because you got a job somebody else wanted). You weren't left alone for a minute—or you were left completely on your own. You couldn't make the computer work. You were assaulted by new sensations. You didn't know where the restrooms and the candy machines were anymore. Even if you love your job, how can you expect yourself not to be stressed out by all this change?

Stress-o-Meter

How many other major changes accompanied your job change? Have you moved? Are you separated from your mate, your friends, your family? Are you searching for a place to live? Is your spouse also taking a new job? Are your children in a new school? Are you searching for a babysitter? Every one of these contributes to your stress, and they may combine to make you regret changing jobs. If people close to you are also subject to these changes, the stress for all of you is contagious, like a bad cold. Is someone in your family ambivalent about this change? Is one of you—or are all of you—homesick? Disoriented by the new place?

If ever there was a time to be gentle on yourself and those close to you, this is that time. Use your support system. Call or write old friends and tell them you miss them. At the same time you acknowledge and accept your regrets, you should also make an effort to meet new people—through church, professional associations, clubs—especially if you have moved to a new town.

Letdown Time

It's inevitable. When you make a change, you're swept along by events for a while, and then you land. It's not unusual to experience a few days of depression. But if the depression hangs on for you or a loved one, consult a doctor.

When you feel you have sorted out some legitimate reservations about your new job, talk to your new boss. Not merely to whine, mind you. You should be ready to present some concrete solutions to any concrete problems you have.

When you leave a job, you get more than just the changes you expected. Everything is shaken up, right down to routine activities like where you eat lunch and how you drive to work. Suddenly, it seems, you're conscious of every detail in your life. A little of that is exhilarating; you can see the world in new ways. But a little goes a long way, and you long for a comfortable old routine. While this time is upsetting, it's also a rare opportunity to change some old habits during this brief moment when you become more keenly aware.

Make Change Work for You

Now is the time to break a bad old habit—coming to work late, for instance. Now is the time to start a good new habit—like taking a walk before work. This time of transition also makes clear how very important it is to give each job change the proper thought—preferably before you take the new job. Misjudging a new job is a difficult mistake to wiggle out of.

The good news is that you're questioning the situation now,

while changes can still be made. You could have chosen to ignore your second thoughts. But count on it, they would have come back to haunt you later.

When you're new on a job, it's easy to get overwhelmed by all you have to learn: the job itself, how to deal with new people, different ways of doing things. Spend your first few weeks establishing routines to manage your workload. Be observant: What you notice now about personalities and office politics will form some of your clearest impressions and can help you avoid dumb mistakes in the future. Stay neutral: While you are still getting to know your co-workers, form your relationships slowly and carefully. Now, as much as at any time in your career, your best course is to keep your behavior businesslike.

Chapter 2

Alienating Your Boss

Follow the advice in this one chapter and you can make 80 percent of your daily aggravations disappear. The reason is simple. Your boss has power over you because you have handed over that power. Some of the boss's power is legitimate: you still have to show up to work, follow orders, and do your job. But there is also plenty of power that belongs to you: you can ask for what you need, you can convince the boss that you are trustworthy, and, most important, you can learn to use the boss-employee relationship. Once you understand how the relationship works, it doesn't matter what kind of boss you have—you will know what to do in just about any situation.

You have been trained from childhood to give authority figures (parents, teachers, clergy) power over you. So even when you grow up and start taking home a paycheck, a little voice in your head is telling you that your boss knows what's best for you, must be obeyed, and maybe even cares about you.

This is not to say that bosses are not good people. Many of them are. But by the time they walk into the office, they are already severely burdened by the unrealistic expectations of all their employees (including you). It's also a good bet that they are overworked and under fantastic pressure from their own bosses. And some bosses are just not competent. Bottom line, most bosses don't have that much time to think about you.

Ready to memorize another important workplace rule, possibly the most important one of all? Repeat after me: *My boss is not my problem . . . my boss is not my problem . . . my boss is not my problem. . . .*

Well, what the heck is the problem then? I'm not going to fall into the trap of saying the problem is you. If I did, you would promptly drop this book and engage in a 20-minute speech about all the wonderful things you do, followed by another 20-minute speech about all the mean things your boss has done to you. So I'll save you 40 minutes right now. You can use that precious time to read another chapter.

The problem is your relationship with your boss. Not who you are, not who the boss is, but how you communicate (or not), build trust (or not), and agree (or not) on how to do the job. If you can accept this premise, we can get you started on how to figure out your boss.

The Career Chat

You're going to use the career chat to help you get to know your boss, and of course to help the boss get to know you. Most of us peons spend less than an hour a year in one-on-one conversation with the boss. That paltry amount of time goes by the name of the performance evaluation. If that's all the time you devoted to reviewing important issues with your significant other, that relationship would be in the Dumpster.

So let's learn how to use the career chat. It's a handy way for you to discuss your job, problems, goals, and ambitions with your boss several times a year. Career chats let you and your boss get to know each other in ways that can enhance your career. It's this simple: The mere fact that you have had contact will make the boss think of you the next time a good slot opens up. Because you made contact with the boss, you will be in her mind. Over the long term, career chats can also enhance your relationship with your boss.

When should you initiate a career chat? You can schedule it about halfway between your regular evaluations. If your evaluation is late (as they often are) or if there is an important matter on your mind, go ahead and schedule it now. A classic time to ask for a career chat is right after a major accomplishment.

Stalking the Wild Boss

Bosses can be wary creatures. Shy and wolflike, they are often suspicious and strive to avoid human contact. So the last thing you want to do is alarm your boss by making your chat sound like something formal. Remember, it's a chat, not the Middle East peace talks.

One way to get around this is to be "spontaneous." Those are not sarcastic quotation marks. What I mean is, set your agenda carefully in your own head, and then you can be spontaneous as all get-out: if the boss's door is open and he appears to be in a breezy mood, just walk in.

Approaching the Timber Wolf

Keep it simple, cordial, and nonthreatening. Big smile, deep breath, "Got a minute?" OK, so you want more than a minute, but you truly must keep it under 15 minutes. That's why we call it a chat.

Monitor the conversation. You do not want it to run long and meander into dangerous waters. Before that can happen, it's your responsibility to observe your boss's reactions, say your piece, ask for a response, and then wind it up: "Well, thanks for letting me tell you what was on my mind." If any follow-up is needed, set it up before you leave.

There are several good reasons for you to take the initiative. Unless you have a remarkable boss, your boss will probably never initiate these chats. Most bosses spend years constructing sturdy, impenetrable burrows out of paper and busywork and other weird, incomprehensible boss-type behaviors.

Another good reason is that taking the initiative allows you to set the agenda. The *last* thing you want is to be hauled into the boss's office because of a problem you could have anticipated and brought up for discussion before it got out of your control.

Eating out of Your Hand

If you have a strained, formal, or bloodless relationship with your boss (as most of us do), you have much to gain from the increased contact career chats can bring—if *you* make sure that contact is civilized, warm, open, and professional.

Once you master the basics of using the career chat to conduct small pieces of career business, you're ready to branch out. Use career chats to also get to know your boss better, from core values to favorite TV shows.

Note to cynics: If you have decided that this is blatant bootlicking, call it what you want. But remember, the object here is to get along better with the person who controls one-third of your life (at a minimum).

TV shows, sports teams, books—concentrate on amiable small talk, the universal lubricant of all relationships. Maybe you and your boss will never become golfing buddies, but you can certainly increase your mutual comfort zone.

Don't Typecast Your Boss

You've probably read one of those books that divides people into types: Bully, Weenie, Loser, and Perfect. Oh, they have more flattering names, but you get the idea. But let's say you think you have already figured out which type your boss is, and you even tried learning the appropriate boss-speak for that type. But you're getting nowhere.

If you are having trouble getting along with your boss, what you really need to know is how to disarm her—a real person, not some type. And, sorry, there is no book that can tell you how to do that.

It Drives Me Crazy

But your boss can tell you exactly what you need to know and often will do just that. Some of them make it easy for you. Listen for these key phrases: "The one thing that drives me crazy is . . ." or "What I really love to see is. . . ." If your boss doesn't spell it out for you like that, you can get the same information by observation.

You are searching for the key to your boss. And here it is: what drives your boss crazy and what makes him happy. Don't look for anything rational, because the key to your boss may be anything but rational.

For example, when was the last time you remember seeing your boss get absolutely furious, at you or anyone else? (If your boss is hot-tempered, your worst problem will be that you have too many examples from which to choose.) The last time your boss got mad might have been when someone was late. OK, now you know your boss hates lateness. Are you getting the picture here? If you tend to be late, stop it. Like magic, your boss will start to defrost.

I Hate It When . . .

Continue to observe what the boss hates. It may be when some-one doesn't show up at a meeting. Or when someone interrupts or contradicts something the boss says. Sometimes it's when some-one makes excuses. Or keeps a sloppy work area. You get the idea. Your boss's extreme response is your cue.

Now, here's the real secret. After you have figured out what your boss hates, make sure you don't do that. Does it matter that your boss ought to be a little looser? Nope, not when it comes to keeping the boss happy. Just be on time. Even if the boss is, in your opinion, a little loopy about these matters, do what you can to keep her happy (as long as it's not illegal or immoral). The way the workplace is set up, the boss is allowed to have quirks. Smart workers indulge them.

You'd be surprised how hard it is for some people to act on that simple rule. Some even seem to take perverse pleasure in ignor-ing those rules; people who are otherwise intelligent and sensitive may even claim they were completely unaware that, say, prompt-ness is important to the boss. Oh, come on now.

Remember, I'm not saying you should put up with verbal abuse or extreme or unacceptable forms of behavior in a boss or anyone else. For those, you must follow your company's procedures for filing a complaint. If all else fails, seek employment elsewhere.

Don't just avoid what your boss hates—figure out what makes him really happy, and humor him. But beware—this may truly gag you. Maybe your boss likes it when you laugh at his jokes, so do (as long as they're not inappropriate). Or compliment something he wears or says or does.

Or if you have observed that your boss is the type of person who has already made up her mind before asking your opinion, then you might as well agree with her. If you strongly disagree, go ahead and voice your objections. But on those matters where the difference in opinion is not that important, just con-cede the point—and watch how the boss warms up to you. In some cases, she will think you're a genius, just because you didn't make an issue. How bad can it be to have your boss think you're a genius?

It's a simple formula, or so I thought. But it turns some people's stomachs to be nice to a boss. After I advised what I thought was merely courtesy toward the boss, a reader from Detroit E-mailed me this challenge:

> "Don't you think that if people spent more time worrying about results and performance, they wouldn't have to spend time worrying about their bosses' idiosyncrasies? It appears that in your article you have given people instructions on how to suck up. Please reassure me that this is not the case."

Results and performance always come first. I do not want to spawn an army of cynical, conniving nonworkers who use my advice to manipulate their co-workers and scheme against their bosses. Ugh. Unclean! I disown you!

Rhythm and Melody

You get into trouble when you think results and relationships are mutually exclusive. When you play piano, one hand plays rhythm and the other hand plays melody. If you only played with one hand, you'd have to sacrifice either rhythm or melody, and the music would not sound right.

At work, results and relationships are connected in the same way. With one hand, you're always doing the best job you can. With the other hand you are using your political skills to clear away obstacles to doing that good job.

Many people think they should not have to pay any attention to their bosses' idiosyncrasies. It shouldn't be that way, they say. No, it shouldn't, and even if every worker made it a point to behave professionally, guess what? We'd *still* have problems at work. And you want to know why? Simply because people's personalities would still grate on each other, because people would still misunderstand each other, because people would still be quick to take offense . . . because people are people.

Just try to get results if you can't get along with your boss. My friend, it ain't gonna happen.

You will quickly run into trouble if you think you can do good work while ignoring the people problems that swirl around your office. You can do a very good job on some project and, with one careless remark, insult a power broker who will then bury your good work. If you're truly clueless, you won't even understand *why* it happened.

Tick, Tick, Tick

I'm not saying you have to devote yourself full time to office politics. That's a waste of time that can keep you from your work. But you do have to understand how the people around you tick—particularly your boss. If your workplace were a car, performance would be the gears and relationships would be the oil. How long would that car run if there were no oil to lubricate the gears? That's about how much work you can get done if you ignore relationships.

Beginners at office psychology stereotype their bosses or co-workers. But that doesn't work, because these people are individuals and deserve to be treated as such. You would hope for the same treatment.

Buying Leverage

There is a payoff. Once you get proficient at doing things the way the boss likes them done, you have bought yourself some leverage. You now have the right to point that out to your boss and use it as a bargaining tool: "Hey, boss, I always keep you fully informed about what I'm doing. Now I need your help. . . ."

So, back to the reader's original question. Does all this politicking and second-guessing amount to sucking up? I say no, as long as your object is to get the job done and do so in a civilized manner.

Are You a Toady?

What's the difference between sucking up and the true care and feeding of your boss? You know it's time to draw the line when you feel you have left your moral comfort zone and are doing or saying things solely to keep the boss happy—or to keep your job.

Some people never question their actions and never ask whether those actions are ethical. They do what needs to be done to survive, and that's that. That's fine, as long as you truly agree with your boss, as long as you share goals and values.

What are some other ways of taking care of your boss? Tell the truth. For example, if a joke makes you feel uncomfortable, say so. You always have the safe alternative of remaining silent, but it gains you little. You just continue to feel uncomfortable, and you can't really expect the boss to change her behavior if you don't speak up (or if you just hope that someone else will speak up).

Make sure your boss knows what's going on. That does not mean informing on co-workers or spreading gossip to improve your position. (That's what a toady would do.) It does mean sharing your observations about morale or productivity, as long as you are not betraying a confidence or putting someone else in an awkward position.

Give your boss praise. And when you do, make sure you explain why. That way, you're not only making the boss feel good, you're passing along information for future use: "That meeting was really helpful. It was good to give people a chance to discuss their worries about the restructuring." A toady would give praise indiscriminately, whether he believes it or not, as a way of stroking the boss. A good boss-maintainer like you gives praise when it is due.

Say no. If you can't go along with something, speak up. Express your reservations. Any healthy relationship includes disagreements from time to time. The toady, of course, can be defined as a yes-person who never contradicts the boss. You are not a toady.

At the other extreme, you may realize that you have fundamental disagreements with your boss. That's considerably more serious than an occasional quarrel between people who otherwise share the same goals and methods.

You may determine that you and your boss agree on very little, that you seldom find anything to praise about your boss, and that your boss does not appreciate the truth as you see it. Then even your best-intended criticisms may only mark you as someone who refuses to get with the program. In that case, you will both be better off if you find a new boss whose values you share.

How to Become the Teacher's Pet

If you have survived so far, if you have successfully managed to keep your boss happy in the basic ways, you're ready for a more advanced lesson. We're going to turn you into the boss's pet.

Does your boss already have a "teacher's pet"? And don't you just want to strangle them both for their cozy, familiar relationship? Hey, any boss who's sane would tell you that there is plenty of room for more pets. You could become one yourself.

Let's assume for this discussion that the boss and the pet are not having a sexual affair, which would muddy the waters of this discussion (and possibly their careers).

Further, let's assume that the boss and the pet do not have a social relationship or any other strong tie that unfairly excludes other employees—although, to be honest, we know that happens. And let's also assume that the abilities of the pet are more or less equal to yours. In other words, let's start this discussion with a level playing field.

Spitball City

So first let's quickly get past the part where you deny that you want to be a boss's pet. "Nah, not me," you say. "I could never stomach being such a brown-noser."

Well, you can view it from that perspective if you prefer, just like you did when you sat in the back of the room shooting spit-balls in fifth grade. Or you can redefine *teacher's pet* in terms more to your liking.

To put it bluntly, what has the pet got that you want? For starters, the boss's attention, a valuable commodity. The pet can walk into the boss's office anytime—while you wait in line.

Here's another priceless benefit: the boss's good will, the lubri-cant that keeps work machines running. Here's how good will can help you. If the boss feels comfortable with you, he will reveal valuable information about what's happening around the com-pany—and how you can pluck opportunities. Or, if you and the boss develop a stronger bond, he may act as a mentor, or point out someone else who can help your career.

Here's how to become the boss's pet. Do your job well—by the boss's standards and by your own. This is the foundation upon which all else is built. Nobody can accuse you of not doing what you're paid to do.

Cultivate the boss's trust. Do what you say you will do—not just once, but over and over. Only a fool would trust you after one good project.

Protect your boss. Before you take any course of action, ask yourself, "How will this affect my boss?" If you think it might embarrass or discredit your boss, consider another action—or take no action. Or—duh!—you could discuss it with your boss first. If this is a surprise to you, you're getting sent back to reme-dial career school, the place where people go when they don't communicate with their bosses or when they make that classic re-mark, "Sorry, it's not my job."

You'd be surprised how many people never even think of how their actions will affect the boss; they can get into tons o' trouble as a result. If you haven't discussed with your boss something that would affect her, why haven't you? It's not just basic courtesy, it's not just professional behavior, it's good defensive behavior.

Strive to make your boss look good. If a project is important to your boss, it should be important to you. Sometimes you can't un-derstand why it's so important. It may even be for crass reasons—for example, the boss will get a bonus. Even if you don't understand exactly why it's so important, that's not the point. You build loyalty by doing those important jobs especially well. You help your boss rise, and a smart boss will do the same for you.

Resolving Conflicts with the Boss

We've all had differences of opinion with our bosses. It's an awkward place to be. But what if that conflict is constant? Here's a message I got from a reader in distress:

> "Please advise me—what is the right way to resolve a conflict with my boss when he is completely in disagreement with my opinion or decision? How should I conduct myself to avoid unpleasant consequences that could jeopardize my job or career?"

It sounds as if the boss may have set up this employee, undermining his initiative and ability to make decisions. And it sounds like a chronic situation. It's a rotten place to be. Here's how to mend the relationship.

Back Off

If your boss is clearly signaling that he wants control over people and operations, then just let him have that control (as long as he isn't doing something unethical or harming employees or customers). We're talking about working within your boss's comfort zone. Your boss's comfort zone for employees making their own decisions might be extremely narrow. But he has his reasons for being controlling, and whether they are legitimate or not, let's allow him that. So you are going to transform yourself into the docile employee he seems to want.

For your own sanity and pride, call it a trial period. Let's say three months. You're going to act like the world's greatest yes-person. You are going to live to keep your boss contented. Just three months. You can hang on that long, can't you, if it may improve your situation in the long run? Sure you can.

Overcommunicate

During this trial period, don't stop thinking, don't stop having initiative. Just consult with your boss before you do anything. Make a conscious effort to communicate, and ask permission before you do anything. This will reassure your boss that he makes the decisions. If this strategy works, you will learn how to suggest your ideas in terms that are acceptable to him, always leaving the final say up to him. If this strategy works, he will begin to accept some of your ideas and use them.

I'm not going to tell you this situation is going to be a picnic, but there is a slim chance that you and your boss will form a workable bond. Your boss will probably continue to hoard the power and glory. While you work for her, you may just have to get used to working in her shadow.

Of course, you're changing your behavior in hopes that at the end of your secret three-month trial period, your boss will finally cut you some slack. The boss's confidence in you (and in himself) may be restored, and he may reach the point where he trusts you more. Even then, discipline yourself to move in tiny increments, always working to maintain your boss's comfort level.

The Gila Monster

Maybe your boss just has it in for you. Sometimes bosses identify one person as a threat. Once that happens, they can sink their teeth into you like a Gila monster and never let go. But even then, being a good boss-maintainer can ease the situation. What's the worst that could happen? Your boss could not change at all, steal your good ideas, and belittle you even more. If that happens, keep on being the world's greatest yes-person while looking for another job, within the company or elsewhere.

Your Boss Doesn't Trust You

Your boss doesn't trust you. How can you tell? Oh, you can tell. Your boss may treat you politely, but you just know something is not right. Maybe your boss excludes you from certain meetings—the ones where the real work gets done or the plum assignments are passed out. You can't prove it, but you have to live with it every working day.

Maybe your boss doesn't ask you for help in tough situations. If she needs something special done, she will ask anyone but you. Oh, she'll ask you to do menial stuff, but never anything that requires initiative.

The Vicious Cycle

Problem is, you want your shot at opportunities to do work that shows off your talent. Those opportunities are going to other people—the ones your boss trusts. Then it becomes a vicious cycle. The boss doesn't call on you, so you never get the opportunity to prove to him that you can do the job as well as (or better than) anyone else, which only reinforces the boss's opinion that you haven't got what it takes.

This is about more than your ego or hurt feelings. Once the vicious cycle is operating, your boss doesn't promote you, doesn't give you raises, and might not even talk to you. Result? Your career is at a standstill.

What to do? For all you know, your boss is not offering you opportunities because she thinks—for some reason—that you do not want them. You probably don't know what your boss thinks about you. So assume the worst—that she thinks you're incompetent—and act your best, working to counteract all bad impressions, even the ones you don't know about.

Volunteer

If you know you can excel at some task, volunteer for it. But pick your shots precisely: if you want to make a positive impression, you must deliver. Over time, as you collect successes, you can build (or rebuild) a reputation for dependability and responsibility, and win over even the most skeptical boss.

Keep at it. You may get turned down, even when you volunteer. Instead of being insulted or discouraged, just keep volunteering. Someday you'll be the only one there when your boss needs a job done, and you'll finally get your chance.

Chat Yourself Up

Use this carefully, or it will backfire: Tell your boss what you did. It's not as good as showing her but it's better than hiding your light under a bushel. Do this at strategic moments. For instance, if you receive a lukewarm evaluation, add a half-page of comments that gently remind your boss of accomplishments she forgot.

Get an Advocate

Is there a colleague of your boss who is a fan of yours? Someone who can talk you up? This is a trump card you cannot use every day, but if you are up for a promotion or otherwise need someone credible to sing your praises, that's the time to ask.

Sometimes nothing works. Call it bad chemistry. You can carry on, wait till this boss moves on, ask for a transfer, or look for work at another company. If it comes to that, remember to check out your new boss for rapport, because now you know how much the lack of it can hold you back.

Serial Bosses

Serial bosses. Just when you get one figured out, they roll in a new one. Here's how a reader named Mark described the problem:

> "Can you give some insight into the trend in which corporations routinely rotate management staff to different project teams at a predetermined interval?
>
> "I work for a data processing department at a large health care provider where management is circulated twice per year on average (same managers, different assignment). The staff is constantly under stress to adapt to (and break in) new management. Differing styles and experience (or lack thereof) are significant barriers to progress.
>
> "This also has a negative impact on morale. Just as we get used to a boss, a change (reorganization) takes place."

If this has ever happened to you, I'm sure you already understand why your company might rotate managers through departments. They may call it cross-training or other management lingo, but it's a valuable tool for giving managers the total view of how the company works, the variety of challenges they may face, and the variety of faces that may challenge them.

But to you, of course, it feels like some new torture devised in management hell—musical hot seats for you, twice a year. Worst case, being rotated through a succession of bosses provides you an unwanted opportunity to offend or disappoint not just one boss, but several.

But let's think positively. Let's turn this experience into management training for *you*.

"Interview" and Make an Ally

At your earliest opportunity, "interview" the new boss about his department of origin. The answers to your questions will teach you more about the big picture at your company and might even open up internal job opportunities that you didn't know about before.

In addition, the mere fact that you are showing interest in this person could make you a new ally and widen the reach of your good will around the company. With multiple bosses, you can have multiple opportunities to practice this "interview" exercise during the year. And when you start putting together the things that each one tells you, you may end up as knowledgeable as any of them.

Next!

If you have had unpleasant experiences with rotating managers in the past, use what you learned to prepare yourself for the next one. You and your co-workers should share a pizza one day and analyze this problem and how you plan to solve it. (See? More management training for you: you're learning about initiative and teamwork.)

Think about whatever problems you encountered when you got your last boss. What can you do differently this time? Bottom line: be ready *before* the next serial boss sets up camp in your department.

Take the Initiative

If one of your rotating managers is the uncommunicative type or gives conflicting or confusing orders, visit the boss as a group. Make it plain that you are there to ask for guidance: "What are your rules? Tell us, and make life easier for all of us."

If your bosses are rotating through every six months or so, don't wait longer than a month to get this guidance. Much more time than that, and you can start getting into trouble. When the boss is new is the time to act.

Gratitude or No Gratitude

If you happen to get a serial boss who is inexperienced, help her to learn about your department. I'm not saying that you should do the manager's work; just look for opportunities to give her some guidance. You will be building loyalty. Wouldn't it be nice to be the one person that manager remembers after moving on?

Oh sure, I can just hear people out there screaming, "They pay me diddly-squat and you're telling me to help out some management drone who's making twice my salary and driving a company car?" Yep. You got that right. And what do you lose if you do spend your time helping out some manipulative freak who will take your help and then just forget about you? You take a chance on people and sometimes it doesn't work out. But sometimes it does. I would take those odds over the lottery any day of the week.

Micromanaged to Death

There is possibly nothing worse than working for a boss who once did the job you are doing now. Try as you might, you can never do it as well as the boss did—in his opinion, anyway. That's the classic example of the micromanager: someone who is convinced he knows the job inside and out, and redoes your work or steps on your toes at every opportunity.

Micromanagers, those bosses who shadow you every step of the way, may not mean to be belittling and frustrating. But they often are. They can destroy initiative and morale and damage productivity.

So how do you handle that micromanaging boss who monitors your every move and sets standards that are well nigh impossible for anyone to meet?

Create Trust

As with anything that has to do with your career, you start by meeting the highest objective standards of work quality, responsibility, and dependability.

That immediately brings up the issue of your boss's standards, which may be impossible for you (or anyone) to meet. That's why you should aim for objective standards, which may be spelled out in your job description, in procedural manuals, or in industry guidelines.

If you concentrate on objective work standards, you are less likely to be undermined by your boss's standards, which may always seem to be shifting upward and out of your grasp. Maintaining specific, reasonable goals will help you keep your sanity no matter how many head games your boss seems to be playing.

Negotiate Terms

You will, of course, need to make some adjustments to your boss's way of working. You can also outfox a micromanager by asking her to meet with you to set out guidelines that you agree upon. Do this immediately. The longer you work without a clear understanding of what is required, the more agony you make for yourself.

Tell your boss you want to have a clear understanding of what is expected of you. Depending on how much your micromanaging boss is breathing down your neck, you can go hour by hour, minute by minute, through your workday. No point is too minor to be covered, and all are important—from what time you are expected to arrive to where you should be at 3:30 every day.

Be cagey. If your boss has done the job you're doing now, ask for advice on how to do it. This is flattering, giving the micromanager a chance to show off his expertise. It also gives you detailed instructions on what to do.

See what you're doing? You're micromanaging the micromanager, outdetailing the detail person. When this meeting is over, both you and your micromanager boss should walk away knowing *exactly* what your job entails.

This meeting accomplishes at least three important things:

1. You know exactly what is expected of you, and you can work toward that.

2. When performance evaluation time rolls around, you have something you can hold in your hand and go over, point by point, with your boss. If you can prove that you met or exceeded the standards you agreed upon, your boss is more likely to honor that agreement. If your boss's standards have shifted since you had your original talk, you can renegotiate standards for the next evaluation period—after the evaluation. Fair is fair, right?

3. Notice I said "guidelines you agreed upon"? That means you pin down your boss on exactly what she expects. That's a job in itself. It also means you do not agree to anything too vague or out of your range of abilities. If you don't know how to do something, this is the time to negotiate yourself some training. And if you can't agree on something, you may be able to reach a compromise by using those objective standards I mentioned above.

Of course, it's not quite so easy as that. Sure, your boss may try to change the standards on you. It's in the very nature of the micromanager. Stay alert for changes in your boss and be ready to make periodic adjustments to your agreed-upon plan.

The Absentee Boss

What's worse than a boss who micromanages your every move? For many, it's the absentee boss. This boss offers no direction, no meetings, infrequent or nonexistent performance evaluations, no decisions. In addition, you will probably not be able to find this boss when you need guidance. (A treacherous variation of the absentee boss is the boss who remains dormant for months on end, then suddenly wakes up and starts taking an intense interest in everything and wrecks everybody's peace of mind, and then returns to hibernation after the crisis has passed. Treat this hybrid boss as both micromanager and absentee boss, as needed.)

What makes an absentee boss? It may be someone who is no longer excited about work. It's a common enough scenario: workers get bumped upstairs to supervisory jobs, farther and farther away from the action. Some of them, the micromanagers, compensate by continuing to do their former jobs instead of managing the work of others.

But others—the absentee bosses—become alienated, uncommunicative, and remote, not only from people, but also from the job itself. Having lost the connection, they may also lose the ability to pass along any wisdom they have. Or, worst case, your boss may be remote because he is incompetent. Until your absentee boss moves on to some other position, you are going to have to manage yourself—and also manage your boss, as needed.

Ask Questions

For starters, if the boss won't come to you, go to the boss. Ask her questions. Keep them as specific and limited as possible, and you may have some chance of getting an answer.

You can also try the multiple-choice approach. If you can't realistically expect true guidance, give your boss two or three choices and ask him to pick one.

But don't turn yourself into a pest. Figure out what you can do on your own, and use alternate sources (co-workers, other supervisors) as much as you can. Where there is an absentee boss, there is usually a "shadow boss," the person who actually gets the work done. Locate and use the shadow boss. When you do go to your absentee boss, it should be with questions that only she can answer.

Set the Agenda

Let's say your boss runs about six months late on your performance appraisal. Your tactic is to get ahead of the process, since your boss will probably not do so.

Find out from your human resources department when your performance evaluation is due, remind your boss of the date, and set an appointment. In the interim, using the form from a past evaluation, write up your own. When you meet with your boss, use your self-evaluation as the outline for the conversation. You can also use it as a framework for any changes you'd like to make in your work situation.

An absentee boss is unlikely to show much interest in your work, so it's up to you to flag your accomplishments. And when you are having trouble, it's up to you to seek help. If your absentee boss can't (or won't) provide that help, find someone who can.

Conflicting Styles

Maybe your boss is not as absent as you think. It may be more a matter of conflicting styles: You feel more comfortable when you get a lot of close supervision, and your boss prefers the hands-off method of supervising. Check with your co-workers. The ones who like to work on their own may thrive with an absentee boss.

If you realize you are mismatched in terms of your need for supervision, you must wean yourself off your need for an attentive, coaching boss. Maybe you'll get lucky next time; for now, train yourself to manage your own work. Fair? Of course not. Real life? You bet.

That's the one thing an absentee boss is good for: if only out of frustration, you will learn to manage your own work life. And that's a valuable gift, even if you get it by default.

You can get along with just about any boss once you accept the fact that the responsibility for the relationship is largely yours.

Once you fall into the trap of waiting for the boss to do something, you're doomed to disappointment. Learn your boss's quirks, and adapt to them. Form the habit of communicating regularly, briefly, and clearly with your boss. Tell the boss what you're doing. Let the boss know when a situation has changed. And let the boss know what you want. You may not always get it, but your track record will certainly be better than if you didn't ask at all.

Chapter 3

Having a Bad Attitude

Let's begin with a very insulting statement: *You are the biggest pest in the whole office.* Yes, I am talking about you. Nobody else. This chapter is my challenge to examine your attitude and improve it.

Tell me if any of these situations sound familiar:

Telling your problems to a thousand people would not even begin to make them go away. . . .

You are sure that there are one or two people devoting all of their time to making you miserable. . . .

You can always find someone else to blame for anything bad that happens to you. . . .

If any or all of the above sound familiar, then you have a bad attitude. Before you even walk in the door of your workplace, that bad attitude has probably already destroyed your chances for succeeding there.

A bad attitude drives away co-workers who might otherwise help you out, because no one likes to be around negative people. It tells your boss that you are a big pain who is not worth her efforts. It blinds you to any of the pleasures of your job, and makes you immune to the many opportunities that come your way—and then pass you by. Worst of all, you've gotten so used to that bad attitude of yours that you may not even notice anymore that you have it. In fact, few people who have bad attitudes would admit it. But they give themselves away by blaming all their problems on other people.

For all your other dreams and schemes to happen, you must begin by taking control of your attitude. First, you have to become aware of what your attitude is—toward work, co-workers, and people in authority—and toward key situations, especially setbacks and disappointments.

How do you know you need an attitude adjustment? Try this attitude quiz.

Attitude Quiz

	Yes	No
1. Are you angry more than half the time you spend at work?	☐	☐
2. Do you think people pick on you?	☐	☐
3. Do you frequently say things like, "That's not my department"?	☐	☐
4. Do you blame others for your failure to move up?	☐	☐
5. Do you frequently say, "That's not the way we used to do things here" or "We did things differently where I used to work"?	☐	☐

	Yes	No

6. Are you convinced that the only people who get ahead are those who cheat, connive, and schmooze their way to success? ☐ ☐

7. Are you frequently frustrated by co-workers or by things that happen at work? ☐ ☐

8. Do you feel powerless to change things? ☐ ☐

9. Do you feel depressed and defeated, sometimes before you even start to do something? ☐ ☐

10. Do you often say, "Yes, but . . ." when someone offers you a suggestion? ☐ ☐

If you answer Yes to even one of these questions, we'll have to assume you have a bad attitude, because any one of these behaviors is probably the tip of a big nasty iceberg. These are all indications of bad attitude.

Classic Myths of the Workplace

Where did that bad attitude begin? Well, many a bad attitude sits on the faulty foundation of mistaken ideas about the way things *ought* to be. The more time you spend grinding away on *ought*, the less time you spend observing how things really work. And if all your attitudes arise from faulty information, you remain stuck in one place, perpetually frustrated and finally worn down.

We all cling to our favorite myths about work. We may quietly hold these myths for years, never stating them, maybe never even being aware of them until they trip up our careers. These myths are often born of a confusion between how things ought to work and how they really work. Myths also reflect a misunderstanding of where power lies and how it is used. You can quickly spot the hapless victims of work myths. "But it's just not fair!" is their national anthem. Here are 10 classic myths about work:

1. *My efforts will be recognized and rewarded.* Keep repeating that to yourself as you watch more people, increasingly younger than you, get raises and promotions, while your desk keeps getting shoved closer to the broom closet. At a cocktail party or other inappropriate place, of course it is pushy to rattle on about your achievements. However, at work it *is* your responsibility—and an exercise in assertiveness—to tell your boss about your accomplishments and to seek raises and promotions.

2. *My boss (the company) has my best interests in mind.* If your boss is also your mentor, this may be true. But if your mentor loses a power struggle, where does that leave you? If your boss is not your mentor (which is more likely the case), he is probably worrying about how to make points with his own boss. And who is "the company" anyway? A group of people, only some of whom work directly with you. True, some companies display a more benevolent attitude than others. But even those companies ultimately make their decisions for economic reasons, not because of you or any other individual worker.

Your supervisor may think she has your best interests in mind—but what if that perception of "your best interests" is based on insufficient information about you? Or an opinion about your talent that is different from your own? The solution: know what's in your best interests, understand what's in the boss's and the company's best interests, and figure out how to make them work together. It won't always work out, but you'll be surprised how often it will.

3. *Management is (or ought to be) rational.* You would be much smarter to say "Management is human." *Human* includes rational behavior, but not always. It also includes prejudices, weaknesses, and other irrational qualities. Under pressure, humans can make bad judgments. Don't expect your boss to be any more rational than you are. And while we're on the subject of rationality, you don't believe that *you're* rational all the time, do you?

4. *I don't need to get involved in office politics.* You must understand the power structure at work, whether you decide to participate or not. And you must understand and follow the basic rules of office behavior, like not undercutting your boss. Do you, for

instance, think the person with the title *department head* is always the boss? Sometimes that is true, but just as often the real power—the power of the budget, or the power to get things done—lies with someone above, below, or sideways. If you don't know who that person is, you need to brush up on your office politics.

5. *Everybody should be treated the same.* That would be nice if it were true, but what really happens? Bosses, being human, are going to like some employees better than others. And some workers, because they know what they want, assert themselves to get it. You can call that unfair, and just pout. Or you can call it the way things work, and start operating under that premise.

6. *I'm indispensable.* All you have to do is go on vacation, get sick, or leave a job to be relieved of this myth. In some particularly tragic cases, all you have to do is show up one morning and find yourself reassigned or pink-slipped, and you will understand that no one is indispensable. You can, however, work to make yourself almost indispensable. The more skills you acquire, in addition to your basic job description, the more indispensable you will become.

7. *If I just do what I'm told (but nothing extra), I'll never get fired.* I recently saw a coffee mug that said, "I have job security. Nobody wants my job." Funny? Yes. True? Nope. What is likely to happen is that person's position will be one of the first to be eliminated, and all those distasteful jobs that she does will be divided among those who remain. There is no job security in doing a so-so job, even if nobody else wants it. These days, you might get fired. So you want to become the person who shows initiative and volunteers for not just more work, but better work. Show your stuff.

8. *Dressing the part will get me ahead.* When the experts advise you to wear clothes for the next promotion you expect to get, there's an implication many people miss: smart workers are positioning themselves by working hard for that next promotion. On them, dressing for success is the outward sign of preparing for success. On anyone who's just bluffing, it's only a costume party.

9. *Things used to be better here.* Yes, there probably was one boss you remember fondly. But too many people utter the deadly

words, "But that's not the way we used to do it . . . ." Nothing is more likely to turn a new boss's stomach than to be compared to a former boss (who probably wasn't as lovable as you remember, anyway). And nothing is as likely to brand you as an unreconstructed relic of the past.

10. *Things will get better.* Some people keep chanting this statement right up until the day the doors slam shut and the entire (very surprised) staff is laid off. If you're not happy where you're working now, find a place to work where you can excel.

Many classic myths of the workplace grow out of an expectation that people in the business world will act toward you as your family and friends do—that is, out of love, trust, and selflessness. But even your family doesn't always operate that way. A functioning family is not just people doing things for you—unless you're still wearing diapers. Even within your family, you take responsibility for yourself and your actions.

While there is certainly room at work for the values of friendship and family, you have to accept the fact that work is a different arena with different requirements. You can't really expect a coworker who wants your job or a supervisor trying to meet a production quota to treat you like family, can you? To rid yourself of these myths, you don't have to become cynical or behave like a cutthroat. But you should learn to work the way the best drivers drive—defensively.

Changing Your Attitude

Changing your attitude is a painstaking process. It is going to require you to be aware of yourself constantly, to listen to the way you talk and think. It's as if you have spent all your life walking bent over, and now you want to straighten up. You will be stretching mental muscles that have been atrophied for years. You're going to have to be patient and firm with yourself. When you catch yourself whining, blaming, or complaining as you did in the

old days, you're going to have to stop, correct yourself, and substitute more positive thoughts and behavior. The payoff is that
you will begin to notice people changing in the way they behave
toward you. They are going to start treating you with more respect, listening to what you say, doing what you ask. And over
time you will treat yourself with more respect too.

It is possible to change. It starts when you become aware of
your own quirks and how they can get in your way; then you can
take steps to change them. My friend Rafael recently noticed that
when he starts cussing more, he makes more mistakes. The
cussing, he said, is a tip-off that he's allowing the frustrations of
his job to rattle him. Then he doesn't think things through (as he
would if he remained calm), and he makes mistakes. So now,
when he hears his obscenity level start to rise, he calms himself
down and focuses his concentration on the work at hand, not the
annoying obstacles.

Talk Yourself into Success

Now that you have an understanding of how your mind can set
you up for failure or success, you can start to make some changes
in your behavior. Here are some of the techniques:

- Start observing your behavior, particularly under stress.
- Listen especially for the remarks you make about people and
  things that make you mad.
- Realize that you can only do so much to change irritating surroundings, circumstances, and people, but you can
  change your own behavior.
- Be patient but firm with yourself, as you would be with a
  small, beloved child.
- Notice how you begin to feel better as you take control of
  and responsibility for your own behavior.
- Notice how all those irritating surroundings, circumstances,
  and people don't seem quite so bad when you exert more
  control over yourself.

Attitude Makeover

You've seen the "Before" and "After" pictures in magazine and newspaper articles—with the help of a hairdresser, makeup artist, and a few borrowed outfits, just about anyone can look better, or at least different. It's fun to imagine what you would look like if you had a makeover of your appearance, but what if you could have an attitude makeover? What needs to be changed, smoothed over, and updated?

Like your appearance, your attitude can deteriorate gradually from a number of bad habits you develop. Just as you can let the heels of your shoes run down, you can let your attitude run down. And, like your shoes, your attitude can reach a point where it is so run down that you might as well throw it away and start fresh. Better to keep it maintained on a regular basis.

Besides making you miserable, a bad attitude shuts you down to the opportunities around you, which you interpret as annoyances and chores. A bad attitude also pollutes the atmosphere around you. It drives others away from you, losing you valuable allies and sources of support. Nobody, not even your biggest fan, can listen to complaining forever.

If You Can't Say Something Nice . . .   An essential step in your makeover is to stop badmouthing. When a negative remark starts to roll off your tongue, swallow it. For a while, people may think you have lost your voice. And then you'll begin to realize how many negative statements have been polluting your mind and the minds of those around you. Misery is contagious. You wouldn't sneeze in someone's face, so don't spread the virus of dissatisfaction to innocent bystanders.

There is no evidence that repetitive or compulsive complaining will relieve your sense of outrage. It does keep your wounds wide open, though. And you know it makes you feel worse, not better; because even if you can get a little sympathy, you continue to feel wronged and angry, no matter how many people you tell.

Which One Are You?

Find yourself among these basic styles of bad attitude:

- *Eeyore*, like the morose character in the Winnie the Pooh stories, is self-critical and pessimistic. For this person, it's never a good day.
- *The Gossip Machine* is always stirring up stories about how other people (always undeserving) are getting ahead by nefarious means.
- *The Nostalgic* moans, "It never used to be like this." For the Nostalgic, there was a golden age at the company, safe in the distant and unattainable past, and ever since then people—everybody else, that is—have been screwing things up.
- *The Critic* doesn't like the way the company is run. Nothing is ever done well enough, and therefore all efforts are worthless. Critics hate the boss, scoff at optimism, and shoot down ideas.
- The person with the *All-Purpose Bad Attitude* sees only one version of reality—his. And it's a very negative reality that never can be fixed.

What all the varieties of bad attitude have in common is that they blame others and avoid taking responsibility. It's always somebody else's fault. In this chapter, we challenge that destructive notion.

After a short practice period of silence, your next exercise is to replace your negative statements with positive statements. You may have to practice reversing negative to positive. For instance, read a positive book or article to inspire you. I keep a computer file of upbeat or funny sayings to cheer me up. You might also keep a photo of someone you love, a picture drawn by your child, or some small trinket in your pocket.

What Do You Envy?   You can stop a nasty habit of criticism if you're willing to search your motives. Ask yourself, "Is there anything I admire or envy about the people I criticize?" (At least for the time you spend struggling with the answer to this one, you won't be actively criticizing.) If you dare to answer it truthfully, you will probably find that irritating person has a job you want or is more comfortable with people than you are. You may have demonized that person, when you could have been observing her to learn how to improve yourself.

Turn Enemies into Allies   Or at least pretend to be civil to them. If you must, you can start this exercise for cynical reasons, like the old saying, "Smile . . . your enemies will wonder what you're up to." But at least be aware that your enemies may be changing as you change. First, think of all the time you have spent obsessing on your enemy's faults, spitefully building your case against him, spreading gossip, nursing your wounds, picking at old scabs. Disgusting, huh? Think of all you could have accomplished if you hadn't devoted yourself to such a worthless, sicko project.

So you start with that smile, and a simple "Good morning." Avoid such dramatic gestures as sending flowers, writing apologies, or sending invitations to your home. This will only draw unnecessary attention or cause the person to suspect your motives. As time goes on, you can work your way up to conversations, keeping them brief at first.

Once you cease the hostilities, you may discover that your "enemy" was puzzled by your frosty behavior or—and this is most humbling—completely unaware of it. You won't believe this now, but in time your former enemy can turn out to be an ally. Most embarrassing of all, in time you may even have trouble remembering what it was about someone that caused you so much grief.

Talk Sense to Yourself   Many of your negative thoughts may be true, but unproductive. Say to yourself, "You're right: Some people *do* get paid better than I do, *do* work less, *do* get promotions they don't deserve, *don't* give me the credit I deserve. That's just the way life is. Now let's move on."

The Cure   In each person's bad attitude style is a clue to the cure. The Critic is a good example. Under this person's critical surface is someone who might love to be in charge, or at the very least have an influence on events.

But the Critic either doesn't want the responsibility or doesn't have the self-confidence to put those critical ideas to the test of reality. And to be perfectly blunt, maybe the Critic wouldn't be much better at running things than the person in charge now. But we'll never know as long as he remains safely in the Critic role, taking potshots instead of taking responsibility.

There are partial solutions to any of the variety of bad attitudes. If you've identified yourself as the Critic, for example, you could volunteer to tackle a specific problem and solve it. This will help you build expertise and confidence. And you will be doing something positive instead of sitting back and criticizing. If, after you give it a genuine try, you find your attitude makeover is not really taking, you must consider that your problems may run deeper than just the habit of bad attitude. What uncomfortable truth about you is hidden behind your bad attitude? Answering this question is like ripping a bandage off a hairy arm, but it's the key to the long-term attitude makeover. You have to acknowledge what's really wrong before you can begin to change.

Turn Negative Energy into Positive Energy   Use your energy to take any complaint or whine apart piece by piece, looking for causes and solutions. In the case of an enemy, for instance, ask yourself some blunt questions:

- Who caused your problem?
- Why did you choose that person to be the focus of your unhappiness? (You did, you know. Why do you think they use the expression "to *make* enemies"?)

- What does your enemy have that you wish you had? A bigger paycheck? The boss's attention and confidence? A lighter workload?

And now for the really tough question: how could you get some of that for yourself? Answering this question takes effort and guts. It forces you to take the focus off your enemy and take some action yourself.

Promotions and raises don't flutter down from the sky. You have to ask for them, sometimes over and over. If that doesn't work, you must be prepared to advance yourself by moving to another department or another company. If you have been suffering from a bad attitude, you probably didn't have the guts to try any of these things. Yes, I am calling you chicken. I'd love to see you prove me wrong. You can do that by building a solid list of skills and accomplishments, and making sure you tell your boss about them. You can build those skills by taking seminars, workshops, and night classes. You can start believing in yourself for the first /time.

If you do all of this, suddenly your complaining quotient will drop. With all that extra effort you're putting into making something of yourself, you won't have much time or energy to complain about others. You'll be working more intensely, you'll be learning in your spare time, and if your efforts don't pan out at your present company, you'll be interviewing for better work elsewhere. Sure, it's a lot of work. It's also risky—there is no guarantee you'll get what you want the first time out.

So why even bother?

Remember that wonderful feeling you got when you didn't have to go to school on a snow day? That feeling of perfect freedom when your whole day belonged to you? Well, when you take the responsibility for your own satisfaction at work, when you free yourself from all the people you thought were ruining your life, you begin to feel as free as you did on that snow day. And all your days will start to belong to you.

Keeping Your New Attitude

You may have to find some new friends. While you are in the process of improving your attitude, you will be most vulnerable to your old partners in crime, the Bad Attitude Gang. These are the people who shared all your bad habits of complaining, blaming, and criticizing.

So now you have to learn how to stay above it all. This is one of the most underrated skills of surviving in the workplace. You will need it now, while you are reforming your bad attitude, but you will also need it later. No matter where you go, there will be another Bad Attitude Gang. These are the people who are quite unhappy and don't mind telling you—and anyone else who will listen—how they've been passed over, misunderstood, and abused for years. Some of them may spend more time complaining than actually working. You don't want to fall back into those habits, especially now that you have started to change them.

Worst case, the Bad Attitude Gang may be lurking right in your work group, making it difficult to get away from them. You, on the other hand, now like your job pretty well and are getting along with the boss. Maybe you're new and are just getting to know your workplace.

Working around unhappy people can be dangerous to your mental health. It's hard to stay upbeat when you spend eight hours a day with people who can and will give you 20 or 30 colorful, well-crafted reasons every day why your job is horrible.

And, like the zombies in those "walking dead" horror movies, your unhappy co-workers cannot exist without feeding off others. They may not even realize they're doing you harm; all they want to do is vent their own frustration. That's about all I can say in their defense, though, because what makes them dangerous to you is that nothing can stop them in their quest to make everyone as discontented as they are. They will knock down doors, come through windows, and stalk you down until you join them in hating work. They just can't stop themselves.

So here's Rule Number 1 of staying above it all: You can't help these unhappy people. Their negativism will drag you down long before you can talk any good sense to them. So don't waste your hard-won positive energy trying to convert or debate them.

What's Wrong with You?

By refusing to join in the general misery, you may subject yourself to suspicion and ostracism. From the point of view of the complainers' group, you have to be neutralized because your very existence threatens them. Translation: If you're not unhappy, then maybe something is wrong with *them*. And they don't want to know that.

To convince themselves that something's wrong with you, they need to find you guilty of some crime they think you committed. So, worst case, in exchange for your good temper you might be eating lunch alone; not invited to parties; and possibly branded as the boss's snitch, whether you are or not. Your ego has to be big enough to resist this pressure. You may lose some people you thought were your friends.

Here are some things you can do to protect yourself. Find new friends at work if you can. If your workplace is too small, then shift your energies to people and activities away from work that support and energize you. Spend more time with your family and friends who have nothing to do with your job. Make those lunch hours less lonely by getting away from the building and doing something healthy. Get involved in volunteer work, take a course, learn a new skill. Let that fill the gap.

Ack! I'm Infected!

At some point, despite your best efforts to avoid it, you may realize that the I-Hate-Work virus has infected you. Now what do you do?

First, figure out what *you* need to do to make *your* work situation better. If something goes wrong in your work life, all the complaining your co-workers have done will suddenly rise to the front of your mind, and you will begin to think, "Maybe they were right." Even if they were, they have paralyzed themselves by resorting to blaming rather than changing bad conditions. Action is what your discontented co-workers reject. But you can take action, and it is the most effective cure for that pervasive feeling that everything and everybody has gone wrong.

If it's time to seek a promotion or a transfer, or just get out of the company, then take steps to do that. Action is the ultimate antidote to the poison spread by the Bad Attitude Gang. The longer you postpone changing matters, the more quickly you will sink into the mud of collective unhappiness.

It's Your Head: What Are You Going to Put into It?

Placing blame and embracing responsibility are the opposite sides of the attitude coin. Placing blame allows you to sit there like a big ol' wart and not do anything. Embracing responsibility means not only embracing the responsibilities of your job, but, more important, it means taking responsibility for your actions (or your inaction). If you choose to do nothing, to remain static, OK. But understand that that's what you're doing, and don't fling blame.

My favorite T-shirt says "Shut up and run." You can customize that idea to almost any situation, but for now it means "Shut up and try."

Changing your attitude will probably be the most difficult task you take on. It requires facing and overcoming some of your most embarrassing character flaws, perhaps for the first time in your life. Who wants to admit that she's a whiner, a blamer, a weasel? But improving your attitude will also offer you many rewards. You will no doubt suffer from attacks of backsliding, in which case you may have to read this chapter a couple more times. Keep your focus on the areas you improve, and build from those.

Chapter 4

Not Having Goals

What Are You Going to Be When You Grow Up?

"Not knowing what you want out of life is a pattern in itself, perhaps the most rigid pattern of all."

—Hunter S. Thompson, *The Fear and Loathing Letters, Vol. I: The Proud Highway*

"You can have your dream if you take your big dream and break it up into little pieces."

—Linda Finch, aviator and businesswoman, who successfully duplicated Amelia Earhart's round-the-world flight in 1997

It's not enough just to do the job; you have to know where you're headed. Too many people say, "I don't know what I want to be when I grow up." They say it in a joking way, but it translates to this: "I don't know how to grow. There is nothing inside me that is pushing to get out. I have no direction. I'm not running my own life."

Sometimes circumstances intervene to give you goals. For example, having a child can shock you into seeing how the passage of time relates to you. And your love for your child may cause you to work harder for someone else than you were ever able to do for yourself. But it's dangerous to wait for something to come along and change your life, because it may never happen.

Now, the Peter Pan types out there may be wondering, "Why do I need goals anyway?"

Goals get you going. Women can drop two dress sizes when they want to fit into that wedding gown. Runners can train when they're tired if they're preparing for a big race. And newspapers would never get out if it weren't for deadlines. These are all specific goals, which must be achieved in a specific time. And when does the weight climb back up again and the nightly run get skipped? When there is no longer a specific goal that must be met at a specific time.

In addition to serving as a powerful source of motivation, your goals can make everyday tasks enjoyable. When you have a goal, work that was drudgery suddenly becomes a game. And when your work is fun, you will perform with increased quality and efficiency.

When setting goals, watch out for these two common mistakes:

1. Making your goal so big that you become overwhelmed and quit
2. Making your goal too small and never really testing yourself

So start small, and once you understand how goals move you on, you can start making bigger ones. Now, be prepared—after you meet your goal, your mind will probably get flabby. You might lose your direction temporarily. Then, of course, it's time to set a new goal.

The Career Goal Checkup

No problem can derail you so completely as a lack of personal direction. In fact, you know you are more than ready for a career goal checkup if you find yourself suffering from several symptomatic problems at once—like procrastination, boredom, poor concentration, and that nasty feeling that you've forgotten something (like your future).

Most of us have not had a career goal checkup since we got out of school, if we even bothered at that time. Then, one day, about the same time we're wondering where that thick midriff came from, we recite the melancholy litany of regret: "When I was in high school, I thought I'd be running my own company . . . writing a novel . . . making my second million by now." You get the picture, and it's not a pretty one. Your career goals, like your car, your health, and your relationships, need regular maintenance.

Fortunately, it's never too late to work toward a goal. My daughter's babysitter has an 83-year-old aunt who just got her master's degree in arts and literature. At every college graduation you can see one or two grandparents in cap and gown. And you know why newspapers love to print those kinds of stories? Because they know the rest of us will read them and say, "There's hope for me too."

There is hope for you too—and you don't have to wait until you're 83. But how do you even remember your goals, or set new ones, when it's been so long since you thought of them? You need a little practice in daydreaming—and some practical steps for making your dreams come true.

Your Ideal Day

To set a goal, you have to admit that you want something. This is very hard for many people, particularly those of us who have been conditioned to settle for what we got.

This exercise will give you some practice in basic relaxation technique while helping you imagine a better life for yourself. Sit quietly and close your eyes. Breathe deeply until you begin to relax. Then just daydream what your ideal day would be, in full detail and vivid color. Let it be as loose and crazy as you want it. Nobody is watching but you.

Your ideal day will probably include a variety of activities, not all of which involve work. It could include a sunrise bike ride along the beach—and living near enough to a beach to take that ride!

Your ideal workday might run, for example, from 11 A.M. to 7 P.M. You might add that you want a half-hour of time by yourself before seeing your family. You might even surprise yourself by saying you prefer working alone, or supervising others, or some other style of working quite different from what you are doing now.

When you're constructing this ideal day, you get to have it all. And why not? Even if you manage to achieve only half of having it all, you're far better off than if you had never asked for any of it in the first place.

An important element of your ideal day should be a sense of satisfaction and balance. In this fantasy, be sure to define what elements of work and nonwork give you pleasure.

Now think about your real-life workday today. Aaaaargh! A hundred irritating people, a thousand dopey little tasks. When the day ends, you look back on all those frustrations without much sense of accomplishment. If this feeling has been going on for some time, only occasionally interrupted by satisfying days, it's not just a fluke. Just so you won't get too depressed, take a minute to remember the positive aspects of your job and your life. Come on now, there must be something!

Compare Your Ideal Day to Today

Are you still cringing because the difference between ideal and real is so dramatic? Fortunately, there is something you can change right now and save your sanity in the short run. Think about it. What changes can you make today, next week, and in the next few months?

Take that bike ride, for instance. Maybe you don't have the beach scenery—yet. Here's your chance to overcome one of the most common self-destructive habits. While you're busy feeling sorry for yourself for what you don't have, you also forget what you do have—and end up doing nothing at all.

So substitute any pleasant nearby neighborhood for that elusive beach. Talk a friend into joining you. You're going to have to get up an hour earlier, sacrificing an hour of sleep. But before you start moaning again, think of the payoff: relaxation, a beautiful view, an increased metabolism, weight loss, cardiovascular fitness, and, perhaps most important of all, something good that you chose to do for yourself. A feeling of control. That's a lot of payoff in exchange for one hour of lost sleep.

Keep the payoff firmly in mind as you begin to add to your list some long-term changes that will require planning, money, training, and cooperation from others. They will take longer to achieve and so you have to keep reminding yourself why you're doing them: more money, more time with your family, better vacations. If it really rings your chimes, it is, by definition, a payoff worth working toward.

Set a Goal

Go ahead. Don't start hyperventilating, just do it. Pick a short-term change (like asking the company to send you to a training seminar) and a related long-term change (like getting your job upgraded to the next level, so you're eligible for a raise and other perks).

Identify Barriers and Problems

If you fantasize about being a trial lawyer, but speaking before groups terrifies you, that's a serious barrier. To find out if it's surmountable, give yourself a small test. Sign up for an adult education public speaking course. If you overcome that fear, then you can consider larger problems, like where you're going to get all that money you'll need for law school. If you hate the course, just be glad you found out now. Then review your ideal day, this time identifying other goals you're more likely to reach.

Set Intermediate Goals and Deadlines

Set intermediate goals that will bring you closer to your long-term goal. For example, if you do decide to go to law school, you have several intermediate goals to consider. Besides studying for your law boards, you must find sources of financial aid, arrange for flexible work hours to fit your class schedule, and locate a dependable babysitter.

For each intermediate goal, set a deadline. Making a progress chart with each goal and its deadline will help keep you on track. Every time you check off one of those goals, you're moving closer to an ideal work situation. It also helps to post this chart where you can see it at least once a day. Something as concrete as a piece of paper with goals written on it can help make the goals themselves more real to you.

When are you ready for your next career goal checkup? Watch for the classic signs of job burnout like sloppiness, grouchiness, and depression. And even if you are generally happy at work, it's a good practice to review your goals at least once a year.

Now That You're All Psyched Up, What Do You Do?

Some time ago, I got a call from a reader who was thinking about making a big change in his work life. He told me he had sold a business, his family was secure financially, and he wanted to try something completely different.

When someone is contemplating a major life change like that, the best advice is to take it very, very slowly. In most cases, if you're thinking about doing something drastic, say, going from a secure but boring bank job to becoming an Olympic luge coach in the Bahamas, that's a signal that something is wrong. Here are some of the possible reasons why you might be thinking this way:

- You're desperately unhappy.
- You're not realistically acknowledging what life can and cannot give you.
- You're going through a life crisis.
- You're avoiding some larger problem with your life, family, goals, or values.
- All of the above.

Many of us treasure the fantasy that we could improve a bad situation by making a dramatic change. Unlike the man who called me, few of us have the means to act on our fantasies. So we keep going as we were and make what adjustments we can, which is the safest course. But if you decide you do want to act on your dream, there are steps you can take to make it come true.

Question Your Motives

Are you experiencing a midlife crisis, which could cause you to devalue the real accomplishments and satisfactions of your life?

Midlife might be defined as a time in which people begin to regret the decisions of their past. Those regrets can occur whether or not those decisions were bad ones.

No matter what your stage of life, are you having other problems that would cause you to want to escape? It's important to assess your state of mind before planning a major change.

Don't Act Alone

You may think it's better to keep your plans to yourself because you don't want anyone to talk you out of them. But you are obliged to consider the consequences of your actions on others in your life. Discuss your ideas frankly with your family and listen to what they have to say. Also, talk to others you trust, but who won't be personally affected by what you do. You need other perspectives besides your own.

Make a Plan

Some people think the only way to make a change is to jump off the cliff, so to speak—quit the job or otherwise force themselves into action. "If I think about it too much, I won't do it" is the rationale here. That's OK if you're willing to be pushed from one crisis to the next, which is not a very mature definition of action.

The fact is, any significant act will require time to complete a series of steps. In other words, a plan. Divide your plan into stages and set deadlines for achieving each one. Planning is hard work. If it doesn't cool your enthusiasm about an unrealistic fantasy, at least it will set you up right to achieve one.

Research

You must figure realistically how much time, money, help, and other resources you will need to achieve each stage of your long-term goal. For some of us, it's important to get that ice water in the face right away: "Law school is going to take *how* long? It's going to cost *how* much?" With those unpleasant but unavoidable facts, we either reject an unrealistic idea or reevaluate and come up with a more reasonable plan.

Ask the Experts

Informational interviews are not just for students anymore. Find out who is already succeeding at what you do and request an interview. A few conversations with established professionals sharing their tips, insights, and experiences can compress an education into a few hours.

Formulate Plan B

Before you set your idea in motion, make yourself a back-up plan. What if you achieve your goal and find it's not all you wanted? What if you discover you have only jumped from one sinking ship to another? In that case, you should either maintain a bridge back to a former job or find ways to alter your new situation to make it more satisfactory.

You're Closer Than You Think

If you've read this far, you may be feeling disheartened by all the prep work. Don't be. Keep working toward your goal. There is nothing more worthwhile than identifying a dream, plotting to get it, and then achieving it.

The One-Year Plan

You are only one year away from just about any career goal you want to achieve. Try the following one-year plan.

What You Must Do Today

By the end of today, you must write down your goal, the intermediate steps you must take, the resources you will need, and the help you must seek from outside sources. This shouldn't take long. In fact, keep this step under an hour.

Your goal doesn't have to be something new. It may be something you've been working up to—or avoiding—for years. But this time, make sure you write down your plans carefully and completely, because they are your first concrete commitment to your goal.

Include subgoals that you must accomplish on a weekly, monthly, and quarterly basis. Your plan must include these intermediate steps and you must honor your deadlines for accomplishing them.

If you can't reach your goal in a year (for example, if your goal is to get a degree in night school or run a department in which you are presently one of the lower life forms), then you can use the one-year plan as the basic building block for a two-year or five-year plan. Keeping your long-term goals in mind, answer the question, *"What can I accomplish in one year?"* The specific answers to that question will form your first one-year plan, with more to follow next year.

To work, your plan should also include a realistic description of any obstacles you anticipate—and how you plan to overcome them.

And don't make the mistake of giving yourself a year to accomplish something that needn't take longer than six months, or three, or two. Instead, make a shorter plan, keeping in mind any larger goals to which it may lead.

One Week

By the end of the first week, take the first step toward your goal. Whatever it is—making a phone call or an appointment, initiating a career chat with your boss—taking action will strengthen your commitment and give you more ideas and subgoals to jot down. Now, and every time you take action toward your goal, make sure you congratulate yourself. This may seem like trivial pop psychology. Do it anyway. You want to associate taking action with pleasurable feelings.

Every Week

Check in on your plan every week. Everyday life—laundry, lunch, just doing your job—can occupy you so much that you forget your plan for days, and then the days grow into months. Use the weekly check-up to renew your commitment and make sure you're taking significant action.

Every Month

For this and every month that follows, your plan should include specific tasks to be accomplished. You should also do a follow-up on previous steps and look ahead to your next goal. Ask yourself, "How am I doing? Have I accomplished what I needed to this month? Did I forget anything? Should I add any steps? Do I need to adjust my goals for next month?"

Every Three Months

By the end of the first quarter of your one-year plan, you should see some visible results. Take a moment to enjoy the accomplishment, then move on. Add new steps and subgoals to your plan if you need to.

Six Months

It's evaluation time. Are you at least halfway to your goal? If not, adjust your subgoals for the remaining six months. It may turn out that your one-year plan takes 14 months to accomplish. Don't fret. Why quibble about being two months past your schedule when six months ago you weren't doing anything? The important thing now is that you're going to make it. Enjoy that feeling.

One Year

Did you get what you wanted? Are you enjoying it? And now, are you ready to set your next one-year goal?

I Misplaced My Goals Somewhere (How to Find Them Again)

It's disheartening to realize that goals you set for yourself are drifting out of your grasp. Many things get in the way: you might have encountered an obstacle and, not finding a solution, just stopped. There are plenty of other things that get in the way of goals, too: illness, unexpected problems, family matters. Sometimes life just gets in the way.

The worst are the trivial reasons. Maybe you just didn't feel like putting in the extra effort one day . . . and then several in a row. The next thing you know, months, years, have passed. Then, of course, besides not having done anything, you feel guilty because you didn't. You may start to avoid even thinking about your goal because you feel like a failure when you do.

Those are some of the ways it happens. Nothing dramatic, just ordinary distractions. But whatever caused you to put aside your goal, you must get back on course. And it happens to be the same way you get busy again working on your goal. Nothing dramatic—you take small, frequent steps toward it, just as you were taking small, frequent steps away from it.

Setbacks

Stuff happens. Don't beat yourself up. Whatever happened, treat it as useful information, adjust your goals to accommodate what happened, and move on.

Those Deadly Lulls

Possibly the only thing worse than a setback is a lull. Lulls are sometimes self-inflicted, and they are sometimes imposed by outside circumstances.

Let's say you had been pushing yourself hard and actually met a subgoal before your deadline. A wicked little voice inside you says, "So take it easy this week." The next thing you know, a month has gone by and you realize you have just lulled yourself right off your schedule. Treat it as a setback, make note of your tendency to self-sabotage, and get back into your plan immediately.

Lulls can also be caused by circumstances beyond your control: someone you need to talk to is on vacation, for instance. But again, it's how you react to a lull that determines whether you stay on course or get lulled into further inaction. If you get stuck, look at your plan and choose a subgoal you can accomplish while you're waiting.

Now, Where Was I?

If it's been a while, you must find the place where you stopped before you can pick up again. Maybe you were taking a course you needed for your job, and it got too hard. You took a grade of "incomplete" and haven't registered for that course—or any other—since then.

Now you know where you stopped, and why. Both of these are important. Before you sign up for the same course and make the same mistakes again, you need to have a frank chat with yourself. Was the course adding too many hours to your schedule? Did you not prepare well enough? Did you find you weren't really interested in the material?

The Big Issues

If your goals remain the same, you must be ready to overcome the obstacles that stopped you before. If you need to sign up for the course again, inquire about tutoring or prerequisites that might make it easier. If you can take some other course that's more interesting and fills the same requirement, do that. It's always easier working on something you enjoy.

Some Good News

But maybe you stopped for a more important reason. Maybe you were taking courses toward an accounting degree and realized you had no aptitude for it. Maybe you found your interests lie in psychology or marketing. At the time, you may have been discouraged by this realization.

Instead, just be glad you figured this out at all. What's worse? Losing a credit and finding a better goal, or trudging ahead to finish something that has no meaning for you?

I must attach one important warning here. If you have a pattern of starting but not finishing, time after time, year after year, you may have more serious problems than not meeting goals. You may need to get counseling to solve that problem.

What Now?

You've figured out where you stopped and why, two important realizations. Whether you decide now to go in the same direction or a different one, take a first smart step in that direction.

A Friend in Need

Locate someone who is experienced in what you want to learn and get some real-life advice. Maybe you wanted to be a professional screenwriter, until you talked to a screenwriter and found out that most screenwriters are not writing a million-dollar hit every year for Hollywood. They teach or work other jobs and write their screenplays in what little spare time they have. Maybe they'll get produced, and maybe they won't. If they get produced, maybe they won't even recognize their work when it's done.

None of this reality checking is meant to discourage you, only to help you set and achieve your goals in a framework of reality, not fantasy.

Step, Step, Step

Now for those small, frequent steps. You were in the habit of not doing something; now you must replace that bad habit with the good habit of doing something. One method is to use a pocket diary to record each step you take. Take some action toward your goal—no matter how small—each day, and record your progress. Working backward from your ultimate goal, write in your intermediate goals at the appropriate intervals. Consult your diary frequently, flipping forward and back, to see how you're doing and determine what needs changing. Anticipate problems and head them off.

The diary gives you a record of how you're doing and when you must complete each task. It also places your goal in the vital context of time. As you're looking at the days in your diary, you won't forget how little there is.

This chapter provided you with a simple framework for developing your goals. But you will soon see that every step you take will reveal new obstacles to overcome. You will need to find your own courage and determination to keep going. That's the part I can't supply for you. What I can suggest is that you stick with the framework I gave you, at least until you get the hang of setting and accomplishing goals. After that, you might customize the framework to suit your needs. You'll know it's working because you will be accomplishing real things, not just busywork.

Chapter 5

Mishandling Conflict

Conflict is everywhere, in the workplace as in life. And many people dislike it so much that they avoid even the tiniest conflicts. What's wrong with that?

Well, for starters, honesty goes right out the window. If somebody has a remarkably dumb idea, most people don't speak up because they know that challenging a bad idea will probably lead to a conflict.

People who avoid conflict get stepped all over. They are the doormats of this world. They don't stand up for their ideas because they would rather avoid the conflict. As a result, their ideas get watered down or tossed out.

There are, of course, people who thrive on conflict. They can sense the people who don't want to make a fuss, and they walk all over them.

Let's say, for the sake of argument, that you are the person who can think of a thousand snappy comebacks to somebody who puts you down—but you don't think of them until hours later when you're tossing and turning in bed, unable to sleep. I'm suggesting that you are a person who needs to learn how to understand and use your anger, not as a weapon but as what it is—a legitimate emotion that can be expressed in constructive and positive ways. Throwing a tantrum is not a legitimate way to use your anger. But at the opposite end of the spectrum (where most of us are), it is just as destructive to sit on your anger.

By not expressing your legitimate anger, you are giving up one important control you have over your life: you are not standing up for yourself. Giving away any legitimate control breeds stress and more pent-up anger.

What Is Conflict?

Let's start with a nice, simple definition of conflict. You and a co-worker disagree on what should be done, or how it should be done. Both of you may have perfectly legitimate reasons for your differing views.

There may also be those muddy elements of power and self-protection in a conflict: one or both of you needs to dominate the situation, just because. Or one or both of you may also feel defensive about your position, and defend it just because you don't want to appear weak or wrong.

But I did promise to keep it simple, didn't I? So we'll stick with the basics: *a conflict is a disagreement.* Conflict becomes a problem when you bring your old baggage—your old anger—to the table. That's when you are either going to dig in and become stubborn out of proportion with the reality of the situation; or, at the other extreme, let the other person roll over you, and leave feeling angry and cheated and, worst of all, powerless.

So let's talk about anger and how it can get in your way. Then you can learn to use anger well.

Understanding and Using Anger

First you have to identify and sort out all your "old" anger. That's what you carry around with you for years, unexpressed, that leads to the destructive slow burn, the tantrum, and the feeling of powerlessness ("I always lose"). Then, when somebody says the wrong thing to you, you express your anger—all of it. You know you're expressing old anger when your response is much more extreme than the situation warrants.

Workplaces of all kinds are filled with irritating people with irritating habits. Even if everybody in an office were a sweetie-pie, the mere condition of working, with its built-in stresses and steadily increasing workloads, makes it easy for otherwise pleasant people to get on each other's nerves.

Low Power, High Frustration

Furthermore, if you happen to be in a support-staff job, frustrations can be even higher, because the power and control of individual workers is relatively low.

I recently read about a study from the University College of London that should give you motivation to take whatever control you can. The researchers queried more than 7,000 people and found that those in lower-level jobs, such as clerical and office support staff, had a 50 percent higher risk of heart disease than administrators. After the researchers had excluded other risk factors like diet and smoking, the one risk that seemed to make a difference for lower-level employees was lack of control on the job.

How do people cope with lack of control and the feeling of powerlessness? One of the sad facts of work life is that when they feel that they are controlled by the system or the boss (whether or not that is true), they tend to strike out at those around them, whether those people deserve it or not.

Useful Defenses

It's possible to reach a point where your feelings about other people (yes, *your* feelings) can endanger your ability to get the next job. Quitting several jobs after a short time begins to look strange on job applications. You can't tell your next employer you quit because someone was bugging you, and pretty soon you will run out of other excuses.

Look Inward

Frequently, when someone is unhappy or frustrated in a situation, he picks one person as a grab-bag scapegoat for all of his frustrations. It's easy enough to find someone to take the role. Look up from your desk and you will probably see three or four close enough to throw a wad of paper at.

But you may notice that this same "problem" keeps popping up no matter where you work. Pay attention to the pattern: the people may change but the role is the same; you decide someone is responsible for all your troubles. If a friend of yours was doing that, wouldn't you become suspicious of the pattern after a while?

Punch Something, Not Somebody

I'm a great advocate of working out the frustrations of work in aerobic ways. If someone or something is burning you up, you have to deal with it right then. It's best to acknowledge that you're angry at the time it happens. This doesn't mean pitching a cup of coffee across the room. It means saying to yourself, "Hey, I'm angry about this."

But if time has passed and you have lost the opportunity to tell the person who made you angry, you still have to expel some of that anger. If you're mad and can't do anything about it, you might as well burn off a few calories. And don't forget the obvious pleasures of hitting a punching bag or a tennis ball and putting an enemy's face on it. By the time you finish a workout, you will feel cleansed, and maybe a little foolish for letting someone get under your skin. Either way, you'll probably feel better.

The Slow Burn

There are plenty of us who say, "Angry? Me? I never get angry." Sorry, but I just don't buy that. There are just too many annoyances in the world.

Let's discuss the slow burn, because it's one way that a lot of people "handle" their anger. They bury it, but believe me, it comes back to stink up the joint. The slow burn is one of the most destructive emotions that infect a workplace. It can poison your attitude and your relationships.

Here's an example of how a slow burn starts: somebody says something that you don't like, say a joking comment on your abilities. Joke or not, you hear it as an insult.

But you don't react. Maybe the time isn't right. Maybe you don't even think about it until you're driving home, when you suddenly remember the remark and say, "Hey! What was *that* supposed to mean?"

Maybe—worst of all—you don't even let the remark sink in. You don't even acknowledge to yourself that you are angry. But it leaves you with a vaguely uncomfortable feeling. The next time you encounter that person, you're going to feel more defensive, and you may not even remember why.

If you don't acknowledge and act upon that unpleasant feeling, you're going to be touchy or sullen, which of course can begin to affect the way other people treat you. They see that you are not approachable, so they begin to avoid you. That's the slow burn.

"I Am Angry"

There's a simple way to stop the slow burn before it ever starts. As soon as you feel angry or hurt or insulted, say so. First, say it to yourself. You have to acknowledge the emotion before you can do anything about it. Often, out of fear or avoidance, we don't even allow ourselves to feel negative emotions in the privacy of our own minds.

The other destructive thing people do with negative emotions is vent them on everybody except the person who caused them. You may tell the whole story to a friend who will try to comfort you but really can't resolve your discomfort. Only you can do that. There's nothing wrong with seeking perspective from someone else, but don't do it until you have first gone to the source of your distress.

As soon as it's appropriate, you should talk to the person who made you angry. Tell her you want a few minutes alone, and then spit it out: "You said I'm always losing files that you need. That made me angry, because I don't think it's true. But if it is a problem, let's resolve it now."

It would be nice if the other person would acknowledge your anger and apologize. But most of us don't want to acknowledge that there even was a conflict, so you can expect a denial. Be ready for it, but don't give up your feelings because somebody is trying to tell you that you don't have them. That's a wicked little mind game, even when they don't realize they are playing it. You know you're angry—your face is flushed, or you are seeing red, or you are breathing hard. That's real. Don't let anyone take that away from you by talking you out of it.

Very likely, the other person may try to downplay the situation or deny that there's a problem: "Oh, I was just kidding. Can't you take a joke?" Without prolonging the confrontation, you should be persistent enough to resolve it. You might say, "From now on, I'll make sure I put files back as soon as I'm done with them." Try to end the conversation on a positive note of cooperation and professionalism. You have aired the problem, but you are also going to do your best to resolve it.

If you're lucky, you will have had a forthright exchange with a co-worker and leave it feeling better than when you started. But it's more likely that everything will not be resolved. So why even bother? Because at least you will have spoken your mind, which will help you see things more clearly.

That Old Anger

Chances are, you got angry in the first place because you have felt slighted in the past, either by the person you confronted or by others. So some of your old anger exploded, along with the present anger. But by expressing this anger now, you have taken an important step. If you start expressing anger at the moment you feel it, you will diminish that nasty store of old anger. You will no longer be shoving anger aside, where it inevitably builds up. So even if this confrontation didn't end perfectly—they seldom do anyway—you will be less angry, and therefore more clear-eyed, for the next conflict.

That old saying that you should not let the sun set on a quarrel is right. Don't let the workday end without trying to resolve a problem. If you don't speak now, you'll have all night to toss and turn and blow the matter completely out of proportion. By morning you could have fretted yourself out of a night's sleep and lost what little perspective you might have had.

The trouble with nursing a slow burn is that you can turn someone into a villain over a small matter. You can launch an unpleasant relationship with someone who will never know why you act so coldly.

So if you're carrying around a bunch of old grudges, it's time to let them go. If, months or years later, you find that you're still brooding about something, it's time to tell yourself to forgive, forget, and move on. It's over.

Sometimes a situation has gone on for so long that you truly can't remember what the first offense was. In that case, you should meditate for a few minutes on how wasteful of your emotions and energy it is to cling to a grudge when you can't even recall why you had it in the first place.

Then, if you can't resolve a slow burn any other way, take symbolic action to end it. Write your gripes, incoherent or otherwise, on a piece of paper and then toss the paper in the fireplace or line the bottom of the birdcage with it. Then turn your back on it and start fresh.

Making Your Anger Work for You

If you're angry at your boss or someone else more powerful than you—which is often the case—you probably just swallow it in the interests of keeping your job. And most of us have trouble just saying straight out that we're angry to anyone, so we usually end up rechanneling anger in unproductive ways like snarky remarks or sloppy work. But who thinks about anger as a positive force on the job? There are ways you can put your anger to work for you.

Acknowledge It

If you try to convince yourself you're not angry when you really are, you accomplish nothing except to put off the inevitable and give yourself a headache in the meantime.

So first, get mad.

Then get analytical:

- What am I going to do about it?
- Does the other person have a valid point?
- Is this really important?

Use It for Fuel

Once you know you're angry, you have tapped into a wonderful source of energy. If you see something wrong, you can fix it, using your anger to motivate you. Instead of sulking (a waste of good anger), you can make some changes.

Let's say one of your colleagues gets a promotion you wanted. It took you months to get your courage up to let the boss know you wanted it, you worked hard on several projects that proved your abilities, you put together a good presentation, and still you got passed over.

You're steamed. Admit it, you are. Disappointed, yes, but also angry.

While you're still plenty mad, formulate a battle plan. How can you win what you want? What did you do wrong that you can change? If you decide you're stymied in your current job, start working on your resume. Every time your energy starts to flag, say to yourself, "I'm not going to sit back and let some other so-and-so pass me by" or "I'm going to find a better job."

Choose Your Battles Wisely

After you've acknowledged you're really ticked off, you can take a deep breath and decide if this is important enough for you to cause a confrontation. Maybe one out of ten times it will be worth the risk. The other nine times, your best course is to play a rough game of racquetball instead.

Choosing your battles wisely is a way of using your power. You can pick a fight over everything that makes you mad, and become known around the office as The Incredible Exploding Person. This gets you nothing; in fact, people will soon have your number and just sidestep you when you start ranting.

Instead, ask yourself, "In the existing state of office politics, what are my chances of winning this battle? And if I win, will I make myself enemies?" These may seem like cold-hearted questions, and they are. There's nothing like a good dose of reality to help you get a grip on your anger.

Work is about building relationships and alliances, not alienating people. If your anger is going to alienate someone, the fight had better be worth it: at least you ought to have a fighting chance of winning.

Goaded into Anger

Once in a while you'll encounter someone who deliberately tries to make you mad as a way of testing you or embarrassing you in front of the boss or your peers. In such a case, just follow the program. Know you're angry, then decide how you're going to handle it. With a cooler head, you can face your tormenter down and foil him. If you let your rage control you, you will do something stupid. If you stay cool, you'll be saying, in effect, "It's not working. You haven't succeeded in making me angry. Let's move on and get some work done."

Let 'er Rip

If you carefully choose when to express your anger, you'll get some attention. Because you have built up a reputation for restraint, you'll have the strategic element of surprise. And you'll say what needs to be said, but no more, because you'll have thought it out in advance.

How to Get Angry

How you handle your anger at work can destroy you, or it can be a powerful tool for building relationships with your co-workers. Yes, I did say "building relationships." You probably fall somewhere near or between two extremes. You hold it in, building a tremendous load of resentment, but you seldom say anything. Your co-workers may have learned they can run right over you because you won't say a word about it. What does it affect them if you smolder, anyway?

At the other extreme, you may be the person who pops off at the least provocation. This behavior leaves you with a reputation as impulsive and out of control. People eventually learn to ignore your tantrums because they're so common. Worse, they may learn to avoid you or work around you.

Anger As a Tool

The key to managing anger is to control how and when you express it. You don't have to give up your anger; you do have to channel it. You can learn to use your anger to propel you to solve the problem.

Let's look at it logically. If you don't tell the other person what is bothering you, you can't really expect her to even know that you're angry, let alone to do anything about it. So expressing your anger in a reasonable fashion is often the first step to solving the problem. The alternative is no change, and more smoldering for you.

Furthermore, if you don't tell the other person you are angry, that puts the entire burden of problem solving on you, and in many cases you may not be able to solve it yourself.

Directed Anger

When you're angry, make sure you tell the right person. How many times have you told everyone in your office how mad you were—everybody, that is, except the person you were angry at? That's a waste of everybody's time. You keep embellishing your story, but no amount of sympathetic listeners can remove the sting. And do you know why? Because you are avoiding a confrontation, probably out of fear.

Don't Wait Too Long

You may talk yourself into waiting until you've cooled down. Then you wait a week, or a year, until you have long since lost the opportunity to speak up.

If your heart is pounding with rage, count to a hundred to cool yourself down. As soon as you are under control enough to say these words—"We need to talk"—say them, and get the other person to agree to meet with you before the day is out, in private.

A Confrontation Primer

Here are some basic rules for expressing your anger to solve problems.

- State the problem. Make yourself as clear as possible. You can do this by limiting what you say to the problem at hand.
- Don't bring up old business. It may be on your mind because you didn't handle it before, but save it. It's past. Stay on point with this problem at this moment.
- Keep it businesslike. Limit your discussion to the work problem that needs to be solved. No accusations, no personal attacks.
- Think before you spew. Consider the impact of your words on the other person. It may feel good to let it rip with no censoring. Save that for the gym or the ride home, or watch "Battling Boyfriends" on a tabloid TV show.
- For now, you must carefully measure your words against how the other person will hear them.
- Equal time: once you have spoken, ask the other person for a response to what you have said, and listen to it. Be prepared to get some anger right back in your face (fair's fair, after all). But if the other person clams up on you out of anger or surprise, it's your obligation to keep the conversation going.

- Keep an open mind. Give the other person a chance to prove his sincerity.
- Work out some solutions together. To get the conversation going, ask, "What are we going to do the next time something like this happens?"
- End on consensus, if possible. Repeat what you managed to agree upon.

Nothing Is Given

By practicing the anger management skills I mentioned above, you have mastered the basics of sticking up for yourself and your ideas in a conflict. So now you know how to fight for yourself in a defensive way. The next lesson is learning to fight for what you want.

One of the most shocking—and valuable—lessons you may ever learn is that nothing is given to you. I have heard this described in a number of different ways. Some people will say, "You have to fight for everything." Others say, "There are no entitlements."

The corollary of this lesson is even more aggravating: even after you have fought and won, you may very well find yourself fighting for the same thing, either with a new person who does not acknowledge your previous victory, or, worse, you may even have to battle repeatedly with the same person over the same issue.

Who Changed the Rules?

For example, every year for the past five years you have gotten a 4 percent raise. Then a new supervisor comes in and gives you a 2 percent raise. Or along comes somebody who doesn't play by the rules as you understand them, and boom! She gets a break that you thought was yours. You haven't changed, but the rules have.

The reason this kind of revelation is shocking for many people is that most of us come to adulthood thinking that there are some things we can count on, like raises, eventual promotions, recognition for our efforts. We believe that our hard work will be rewarded.

What is going on here, anyway? Author and physician Andrew Weil said in a recent radio interview that we live in an era of probabilities, not certainties. Some would say that this uncertainty is a by-product of corporate turmoil, reorganization, and downsizing. Or it might be a result of the rapidly accelerating change in the world of information. Those forces certainly exaggerate our sense of uncertainty, but it didn't just start with them. It was always there.

The bald fact remains: if you believe good things will come to you in good time at work, you are bound to be disappointed. Worse, you might be one of the people who are downsized—and you'll never know what hit you, or why.

How you react to the realization is what can save you. When something bad happens to some people, they just deny that it happened. Others become bitter and learn to blame their setbacks on forces beyond their control. In both cases, they are doomed as long as they do not learn to adjust and do not act.

Not Easy, Not Fair

The people who survive the era of uncertainty are those who say, "Oh, so this is how it's going to be. Things aren't going to be easy and they aren't going to be fair. Well, I guess I'll adjust my strategy." Does this mean you become cynical and conniving? Does it mean you stop playing by the rules and start playing by the numbers? No. It does mean that you augment your basic job skills (the ones in your job description) with some survival strategies. You learn how to anticipate, and you steel yourself to keep on fighting until you get what you want.

Think again about what Andrew Weil said: probabilities, not certainties. At first, this may be discouraging—probabilities seem limitless—but in fact it's the key. Starting now, you can analyze almost any situation in terms of its probabilities. Let's say you get a new boss. If you are inclined to think in terms of certainties, you will say, "Things will be the same." If, however, you think in terms of probabilities, you will say, "That is only one of several probabilities, and since bosses manage in different ways, it's not a very likely one."

Now you have the idea. You can pick probable scenarios: the new boss may review everyone, rearrange the department, pick one or two people to rely on, or all of the above. Based on any of those probable actions, you can anticipate how you will act.

Here's another example: You have just been promoted. You have plans to make things better. But surprise—people don't necessarily do what you expect them to (and that may even include your bosses as well as your employees). You thought you had power, only to find that you have to jockey and connive to get even the simplest thing done.

Accept the reality of change. Anticipate outcomes. Act on what you have learned. And when things don't go your way, just keep fighting for what you deserve until you get it.

Big Important Rule

Since nothing is ever handed to you, you must stay in a constant negotiating frame of mind. Every day, every conversation with a co-worker is an opportunity to horse trade for something that benefits you both. Is this a lot of work? At first, yes. You have to learn what your co-workers want, and that takes time and observational skills. But after a while, horse trading and looking for opportunities can become second nature.

Horse Trading 101: Basic Negotiating Skills

Negotiation is a wonderful way to resolve conflicts. People usually think about negotiation in a limited way—that it's what you do when you're buying a car. In fact, negotiating is built on a simple premise that goes on hundreds of times in every workplace every day. You want something and I want something. What you want and what I want seem to be in opposition; but if we negotiate, we can find what we have in common and both of us can leave the table with something we want.

These skills will only work if you start from the basic premise, "I'm worth it." The very act of negotiating requires you to open up your mouth and say what you're worth.

Next, you have to be wise enough to give as well as take. Sometimes it works to negotiate like Attila the Hun: "Give me what I want or I will burn your village to the ground." But most of the time you have to be a little more subtle than that: "I have something you want (now you have their interest!) and, oh, by the way, you have something I want. Let's see what we can work out."

The other thing to remember about negotiating is that it's not just something you do under special circumstances, like asking for a raise. Negotiation is an attitude: How can we help each other out? How can we give something to get something? And if you're not using that attitude every day, you are missing opportunities.

Sure, you negotiate with your boss over that raise. But you can also negotiate with your colleagues about sharing the workload, and you can use negotiation tactics to resolve conflicts and problems that arise every day.

Why do most people advising you on how to negotiate tell you that it's important for both sides to feel they have won something? If you find that idea peculiar, then you probably also think that the whole point of negotiating is to pound your adversary into the ground, get everything you want, and step on his head on your way out the door.

Well, it's not. And if you think that, you're probably an awful negotiator. You'll do much better if you think of yourself as a diplomat instead. If you treat negotiation as war, then when you win, you also win a new enemy, which nobody needs. Enemies don't forget. Neither do friends. So you might as well win a friend with whatever else you win while negotiating.

Let's talk about the joys of negotiating. Not only is it not war, but it needn't be that loathsome a chore either. If you let it, it might even be a growth experience for you. So you owe it to yourself to get better at it.

This is negotiating: Know what you want. Know what you will give to get what you want. Know what you will not give. And know when to walk away.

Negotiating Is Forever

Stop thinking about sides. Think instead about the other person as someone you want to get along with for a long time. Then, suddenly, you have changed the whole tone of negotiating. That's not just a mental trick; it's truth. In most cases, you're negotiating with someone you work with or live with, someone you need to cooperate with, if only to make your lives easier.

Go Ahead, Ask

Somebody wise once said to me, "If you don't ask, you don't get." Words to negotiate by. Unfortunately, most of us were brought up to take what we're offered and shut up. So the very act of speaking up and saying what you want is an alien concept.

Then, one day, maybe by accident, you ask for what you want. And you get it. Oh, joy! This happened to me when I was a free-lance writer. A client called with a job I just did not want to do. When the client asked me how much I charged for my work, I heard myself doubling my usual fee, hoping to get rid of her. Then—surprise—the client cheerfully agreed to pay the fee, and later praised my work. Go figure.

After an exhilarating moment like that, you're never the same. Once you've gotten something you want, it's a short step to wanting and getting more. And that's definitely a growth experience.

And What Will You Give?

Kids are often better negotiators than adults. Listen to them negotiating among themselves, and you can tell that they instinctively understand the back-and-forth process of negotiating very well. They probe every aspect of the deal, looking for an opportunity to change the terms in their favor. At the age of two, my daughter was already learning to negotiate. She started her proposals in a nonthreatening way: "How about . . ." and ended with the equally reasonable "Is that fair?" She's still that way. She gives, she takes, she deals.

But that same fine probing quality that allows children to negotiate complex trades of sports equipment and toys among themselves breaks down the moment they run up against an adult who has only two standard responses: "No" and "Because I said so." Those are two fine answers when a situation is dangerous or unacceptable. But for the other 80 percent of the time, parents and children could successfully negotiate all sorts of matters. And so could the rest of us—co-workers, bosses, and employees.

To be a good negotiator, you have to know the following things before you begin:

1. What you want
2. How far you're willing to go to get it
3. What you'll give up
4. What you won't do to get it
5. When you are willing to walk away from the deal

I Don't Need It

This is a great negotiating stance, but it's not an easy one. I learned this from a boss of mine a long time ago. He was talking about how he went into a very tough negotiating situation. "I asked myself, 'Can I walk away from this job if I have to?' And the answer was yes."

By doing this, he defined the extreme terms of the negotiation process—what he was willing to give up if he had to. A lot of the fear goes away when you face the worst possible outcome and decide you can live with it.

You have to convince yourself that you don't need whatever it is. You want it, yes, but you won't die if you don't get it. If you can absorb this radical thought, you transform yourself from a beggar into a negotiator. You can then determine what *your* terms are.

The other secret to negotiating is knowing when to walk away from a deal. Another smart person once told me, "You have to know what you absolutely will not accept." The details are up to you: it could be anything from the lowest salary you'll take for a job to how much freedom you should have in your work. Going into any deal, you may not yet know what you will not accept. But when you hear it, you'll recognize it. When an alarm goes off in your head, pay attention to it. Remember, you don't need it, right?

Breaking the Conflict Cycle

You only get good at negotiating by practicing it. Fortunately, you will probably have several opportunities to hone your negotiating skills in any workday. For the next few days, look at any conflict, any problem, as an opportunity to negotiate. And remember that the object of negotiating is for both you and the other person to get something you need.

You won't stop having conflicts once you get into the negotiating frame of mind. But you will resolve them more frequently and more happily. And you will break out of that nasty cycle of anger and powerlessness. Here's how it works. Because you have stood up for yourself, you are not going to be angry—the slow burn kind of anger—as often. And when you are not jerked around so often by your own anger, you'll have a cooler head. When you have a cooler head, you'll observe situations more astutely, and your judgment will improve. You will not pick fights at the wrong time or beat yourself up over the fights you backed out of.

Yes, it's true. By becoming a good negotiator, you will be happier at work.

Conflict is a natural process, at work as in anything else you do with other people. If you think you can avoid conflict, you're wrong. You'll just find people walking over you, which will leave you feeling more and more angry and resentful. First, face your anger; then learn how to use it in negotiations. You don't have to win every conflict, but you do have to stand up for your views. If you learn to do that, you can become a powerful negotiator.

Chapter 6

Misplaying Office Politics

If you're looking for one good reason why you need to understand and master the basics of office politics, here it is. No matter how smart and competent you are, no matter how unique your ideas, you will not thrive in your workplace if you can't get people to cooperate with you. Furthermore, if you alienate those around you for whatever reason—you decide they are stupid, in-competent, or disloyal—they will eventually bring you down, and all your efforts will be for nothing. And even if you profess to have no ambitions, if you're one of those people who just want to do the job and get home, you still need skills in office politics. Why? Because those who are ignorant of office politics can be crushed by it anyway.

You may be thinking, "That's all very well for managers, but I'm just a foot soldier. What has it got to do with me?" Of course it's a manager's job to get others to act on her ideas.

But before you reach a hasty conclusion that this has nothing to do with your effectiveness, take a look at these characteristics of people who fail at office politics. Some or all of them may apply to you.

- *Impatience.* You may be quick to figure things out, but you can't expect others to be able to do the same—or to be able to read your mind. As a general rule, the faster your mind works, the more important it is to slow down, listen, and wait before acting.
- *Poor communication.* Instead of thinking that the other person is just thick-headed (which may not be true at all), concentrate on improving your methods of communicating your ideas. Do you repeat ideas or instructions in at least a couple of different ways? Do you translate them into terms other people understand? Do you ask others to tell you which parts don't make sense? Do you encourage questions?

You need to take full responsibility for what comes out of your mouth; that means you should make sure it arrives more or less intact in the other person's brain.

- *Ignoring the power people.* In every company, every institution, there are people who have titles—and then there are the people who make things happen. They may be the same people, and they may not. They also are the people who can stop things from happening if they do not share your vision, or, worse, if they just don't like you.

If you truly want to accomplish things, part of your job is to identify the people with power and influence and identify which areas they control. Even if you are powerful, say a department head, you will not be able to accomplish your agenda if other key power people are not working with you, or if they are actively working against you.

• *Isolation.* Identifying power people is not just a cynical exercise in manipulation. Among the power people are those who can be your allies, advising you and steering you away from stupid and costly mistakes. You will only find them if you are making a genuine effort to get to know people. If you refuse to get to know people, if you isolate yourself, you will be far less effective.

• *Breaking the rules.* You may think that merely stating what you want to do is equal to getting it done. This is naive. Once you enter an established power structure, you have to figure out what the rules are, what territory is being jealously guarded, and whose toes you may be stepping on. Then, anything you do must be done in that context, or you will be identified as an outsider, even a troublemaker. People will find ways to cut you out of decisions, ignore you, or undercut you.

If you're the boss, you are not immune from politics either. Even if you're in a position to fire everyone who disagrees with you, you'll be more effective if you take the time to map out the political territory around you.

Let's say you need a letter typed now and your assistant is out of the office. You may think there's nothing wrong with asking someone else's assistant to do it for you. The assistant might even do what you ask.

But chances are, in getting your letter typed quickly, you have managed to alienate two people—the assistant, whom you put in an awkward position, and the assistant's boss, whom you should have asked first. You may even have managed to offend your own assistant, who could interpret the incident to mean you decided someone else could do a better job.

Does this seem bizarre, like a foreign country with its own rules? It is, but you're stuck with it. There is a payoff, however: once you learn the rules, you'll be much more effective at bending them when you need to.

The Good Boys and Girls—
and How to Stop Being One

You may fall into another category of people who are crushed by office politics: the Good Boys and Girls. Take this test and see if you might be one of them.

	True	False
1. No matter how trapped you feel in your present job, you would feel disloyal, almost adulterous, if you interviewed with another company.	☐	☐
2. You are appalled when you hear that your boss made a promise and didn't keep it.	☐	☐
3. You will speak up even when you know your views are controversial.	☐	☐
4. Your friendships with co-workers are more important than your ambitions, and you hope they feel the same about you.	☐	☐
5. You are often shocked by what people do to get ahead with your company.	☐	☐
6. Over and over, you see the loudmouths and egomaniacs get all the raises and promotions. People get rewarded for reasons that seem unfair to you.	☐	☐
7. You believe that if you work hard and don't complain, you will be rewarded. That reward just seems to be taking a long time to arrive.	☐	☐
8. You would never do anything that might harm someone else, even if it might help you get ahead.	☐	☐

	True	False
9. Playing the office politics game is repulsive to you.	☐	☐
10. You act for reasons of principle, not for reasons of practicality.	☐	☐

If you think those statements are true, you may be suffering from Good Boy/Good Girl Syndrome (GBGGS). People with GBGGS think that there is only one set of behaviors to be used both at home and at work. What other people call career strategy, Good Boys and Girls label as amoral, selfish behavior. While Good Boys and Girls wait patiently for the rewards they've earned, they're secretly worried that those rewards will never come.

Our parents and teachers taught us to be Good Boys and Girls. The message was, we will be pleased with you if you get good grades, don't make a fuss, and stay out of trouble.

But your boss is not your parent, and your co-workers are not your brothers and sisters or aunts and uncles. And until you realize that, you can be victimized and frustrated by a system that rolls right over the Good Boys and Girls.

To get over GBGGS, you don't have to turn into a lying, cold-hearted shark. But you should start viewing your relationships at work in a different way. You can't really expect people at work to love you like family.

Just as you pay the dry cleaners for a service, your boss pays you for your services at work. Generally, you're evaluated by your boss and others on your ability to deliver those services.

You may be uncomfortable with the notion that work is no more than trading money for service. You may feel you would be false to your beliefs if you put on a different personality at work. Think of it instead as a kind of role-playing. You reveal those aspects of your personality that enhance your work and your image as a worker. You keep the rest of your personality to yourself. It's not so much a compromise as a process of selecting what to show.

Actor Gregory Hines said in an interview that he wanted a role in the movie *Cotton Club* so much that he visited producer Robert Evans in vintage clothing and tap-danced on Evans's coffee table. Evans hired him. "I decided then and there that if there's something I really want I've got to go for it," said Hines. "And the aggressiveness, I figured, why not? I'm not trying to develop a relationship with these people—that comes after you get hired. What I'm trying to do is convince them that I'm the man for the job."

You, too, can play the role that gets you what you want at work, be it money, respect, responsibility, or all of the above. But you have to start thinking of yourself as the person who will get all of that for you.

If some magical boss finally did grant you all that you deserve at work, what would it be? From now on, keep those wishes firmly in the front of your mind, and concentrate on how you, not some fairy godmother, can make your dreams come true.

Your needs and ambitions are as important as anyone else's. Train yourself to speak up when you want something.

Practice thinking of your job skills as resources that are worth money to more than one company.

When you catch yourself thinking, "I'm lucky to have a job," also tell yourself, "They're lucky to have me working here."

As a regular exercise, evaluate shakeups, promotions, and new hires first in terms of how they affect your position at work. Then you may consider how they affect your friends.

Be a good listener. You'll learn more by listening than by talking. Let others plant their feet in their mouths.

Keep secrets. Don't volunteer what you know unless you plan to trade your information for something you need. What you know belongs to you.

Don't lie, but at least say as little as possible.

Don't expect people at work to look out for you. Then, when it sometimes happens that they do, you'll be pleasantly surprised.

Continue to look for opportunities to help others. If you have information that can benefit someone else, pass it on—after you've determined that it won't harm anyone or break a confidence to reveal it. One way to build loyalty and alliances is to look out for others. That's politics, it's just not the cutthroat kind of politics.

Still Politically Impaired? Get a Mentor

If you are clueless about what goes on in your office, you need to get yourself a mentor. Look around the room for someone who has been in the business a few years, understands the dynamics and the players, and would be willing to share some of that political expertise with you.

There are probably several people who fill that bill. Before you approach anyone, do a little homework to find out anything that you need to know about your potential mentors, like whether they drink a bit too much or like to sleep with their protégés. Your eyes should be open before you enter a mentor relationship, which works best on openness and trust. You don't want any nasty surprises.

Once you've done your research, you may have to approach all of your candidates before you find one person who seems to click with you. If you find more than one, you are lucky. Keep all the willing mentors you find.

Bad Mentors

There are some mentors you should stay away from, however. Those are the people who are embittered or out of power. They may have a lot of knowledge to share, but the price you pay will probably be too high. You could be poisoned by their unhappiness faster than you can learn from them. Another serious risk: by associating yourself with an "out," you run the risk of being labeled one too.

Teamwork for Loners

Now we're going to talk about teamwork. This session is absolutely required for lone wolves and people who sneer, "Right. We're a team just long enough for you to get what you want," or something equally cynical.

Those of you who are true believers in the idea of teamwork can skip this class, but wait just one minute! You have homework. You must locate a lone wolf in your office and find a way to recruit him to your team. That ought to keep you busy for a while.

So, those of you remaining in class, please don't think I'm just picking on you. You probably feel as if you've already heard a lot of cheap talk about teamwork; but tell me, do you know what's really so important about it?

If you're the type of person who prefers to work alone, teamwork seems like dragging your feet when you could be galloping ahead of the pack. You're quick to pick up on things yourself; you're impatient with how long it takes others to learn. If you're honest, you'll admit you don't value the opinions of others. You may not even stop to listen to them.

The mistake loners usually make is to trust themselves to a fault and to ignore others as a resource. Loners often convince themselves that since they are smart, they have nothing to learn from others. No matter how smart you may be, that person sitting next to you has a different way of looking at things. Different may or may not be better, but it can at least be thought-provoking. The more thought, the more discussion, the sounder the ultimate course you choose.

You can learn something from that different perspective, but only if you listen. You may even have to take the initiative: ask what he thinks.

There are many times when you really can't accomplish as much alone as you could with others. But before you can acknowledge that truth, you have to let in the notion that other people have ideas as good as yours. If you are cocky, or if you are not too confident or comfortable cooperating, this will be hard for you. Some people prefer to work alone for no better reason than because they just don't know how to work with others. Over time it becomes "easier" to work alone than to figure out the give-and-take of cooperation.

The Big Picture

You also need to have a larger view of what's important at work. Larger than what, you may ask? Larger than your own vision, for instance. Few of us are talented at seeing the long view, the big picture—and fewer still know how to make it come to pass.

Ego? Me?

Then of course there's the whole problem of ego. That's the part of you that wants to take the credit, wants to be in control, doesn't want to share the glory. Those are all normal impulses unless they crowd out other important goals like doing the best possible job.

Energy Building

A good team is also good for everyone in it. Workers who are committed to a team are more likely to work beyond their job descriptions and to be more satisfied with the work environment, according to a recent study done by professors Robert Billings of the Ohio State University and Thomas Becker of Washington State University.

Can You Change?

If you have ever taken one of the many tests that tell you what your "work style" is, you probably think, "I'm a loner, that's what I'll always be. I can't change." True, you probably will revert to loner style in a crisis, but you can teach yourself some teamwork skills.

Make it a practice to ask others for solutions, even if you think you already know the answer. Ask them for their opinions and then listen closely to what they say.

What's Missing?

The other thing you need to acknowledge is the gaps in your expertise. Every team needs an array of talents, which almost by definition has to be supplied by a variety of people. A team needs an idea person, an optimist, a detail person, a negotiator, an enforcer, and some faithful followers, just to name a few.

Once you know which of those is your talent (and which is your weakness), you can start hunting for others to fill in the blanks. A smart team builder will locate those people and form a team with them. The interlocking talent pool can be awesome.

Office Politics Is Not War

A lot of people think office politics is just a civilized-sounding name for discrediting or destroying their enemies. What they don't understand is that it is foolish to make enemies in the first place. You will get a lot farther if you start by redefining what the enemy is.

Every once in a while, it becomes fashionable again to apply the metaphors of war to the workplace. Managers study dog-eared copies of Sun Tzu's *The Art of War* or whatever is the latest business book based on combat strategies, and they find ways to translate warlike ideas to work. Is that a problem? Well, it sure can be when people forget who they're fighting and what they're fighting for.

When that happens, the warrior techniques remain, but the enemy becomes the person in the pod next door. The next thing you know, you're using all your best energies to damage someone within your organization. If everyone starts playing war games, the effect on the organization is very destructive. And if you are thinking, "Who cares?" I'll give you some reasons to care:

1. If you contribute to a warlike atmosphere, you will eventually become its victim. You may be in the "in" group now, but when someone else is in (and eventually, someone will be), you will be brought down.
2. The more obsessed you are with working on your warlike skills, the more your real job skills will suffer.
3. Your reduced competence will be one of the reasons cited by the new "in" group when they reassign you to the broom closet.

Warlike Words

Let's talk about how you got in this mess in the first place and how you can extract yourself. Warlike ideas have long been part of the lingo of managers, who use such words as *campaign, objective, strategy,* and other terms that suggest generals at war. Managers also like to cast the competition as the enemy, using the good old desire to dominate as a tool for motivating their troops. (Troops. See how easy it is to fall into warlike ways of thinking?)

How does it happen that people get distracted from conquering an outside enemy and start fighting among themselves at work? Basic human emotions like fear and anger get turned into backbiting, infighting, gossiping, and rumor campaigns. Jealousy and grudges continue for years past the original fight. Next thing you know, everybody is locked into factions and the battle can rage on for years.

Some people get too much of their sense of identity from work, and lose their sense of proportion. They begin to obsess on how every little change in the organization can affect them. For them, it's only a small step from becoming defensive to using outright offensive tactics against someone else. If one of those offensive, warlike people happens to be the boss, your task of remaining neutral is just that much harder.

Sound familiar? You bet. Are you comfortable working in that kind of atmosphere? Well, a few people thrive on intrigues, but the rest of us don't. When people start using such techniques, it soon contributes to a toxic workplace. And such shenanigans distract everybody from doing a good job.

Symptoms of Trouble

Some of the symptoms that show you are engaging in warlike behavior: deliberately making someone look bad to improve your own image; going along with an idea because you're loyal, and not questioning whether it's really a good idea; talking negatively about a co-worker or just plain making fun of him; throwing obstacles in the way of someone else's idea just because it's not yours.

Removing yourself from a warlike frame of mind is not easy. Some people cannot function without casting someone as the enemy and using their energies to destroy her. If you are feeling squeamish about all of this, though, that's a good sign. You have a chance to change.

1. Start catching yourself when you're displaying the symptoms mentioned above. Stop allowing yourself to use these nasty games. Recognize them for the fear-driven, cowardly tactics that they are.

2. You will be most likely to backslide in the presence of your warlike colleagues, so steel yourself to remain pleasant but neutral.

3. Redefine *who* you're fighting as *what* you're fighting for. Take the personalities out of it, concentrating on skills and goals.

4. Keep your vision. Once you know what you are fighting for, it will be easier to stick to it.

5. When challenged by a warlike person, refuse to engage on his terms. That means having the character to shrug off the put-downs, and the resourcefulness to combat the snaky

tricks. After all, the wisest warrior can find a way around any obstacle.

What Is Power, Anyway?

It's great to fantasize about what you would do if you ever got your hands on some power. When you actually do get some, it's not nearly so much fun. It feels more like responsibility.

In the fantasy you can use power like a weapon ("Off with their heads!"), but in real life it's just another tool, like a computer or a screwdriver. Or a car: something you use to get you where you need to go.

The Fear Factor

Take fear, for example. If you have power, people are afraid of you, even if it's only in the back of their minds and even if it's not immediately visible to you. They are afraid that you could fire them or otherwise make their lives miserable.

If you care to, you can certainly crank up the fear level of those who work for you. You can regularly use disciplinary measures, you can make stern speeches. You can set tough standards, and then, if necessary, crack some heads when people don't meet those standards. Nothing wrong with any of that, as long as it's for the right reasons. (If you notice that you truly enjoy having people fear you, that's a wrong reason. Power is not synonymous with sadism.)

Certainly you should make your standards clear and hold your workers to them. And discipline those who fail to meet them. In fact, to maintain your power, you must do that. If you do not enforce consequences, people soon realize that they don't have to do what you tell them, and your power will disappear like water out of a sieve.

Fear can work as a short-term tool. For instance, fear can focus the attention of workers who can't seem to meet work standards on their own, when no other tactic of yours is working.

What won't work very well is to create a climate of fearfulness. Ultimately fear wears people down, robs them of their initiative, builds resentment, and erodes the quality of the work.

That's another one of the disillusioning facts about power. You have the power of fear, but you can't use it that often, certainly not on a daily basis. You still have to use persuasion, which takes more skill and patience.

Losing Power

Just as you can erode your power by not enforcing consequences, you can lose it in other ways. For instance, if you allow yourself to get distracted from your goals, you give up the power that those goals contain. And the same lack of focus will surely trickle down to the people who work for you. They too will get lost in trivial details.

One of the worst things you can do to erode your power is to misunderstand the consequences of your actions. If you are heedless of the effect you have on those around you, you are not using that power properly.

You may have power that you are unaware of. For instance, people may look to you for guidance, a good example, and the wisdom and perspective they lack. You need to use that power. But you may fail to use your power because you don't understand what you are supposed to do with it.

Let It Be

Possibly the best tactic of all is to know when not to use your power. That's right, you have to know when to step back. If you like to control things, this will be the toughest trick for you to master. Managing people means guiding them just enough to let them succeed on their own. It's much harder to let them alone long enough to struggle and learn and master their jobs. People need to feel that they have enough room to do that.

That certainly doesn't mean that you disappear for weeks on end. Maintaining communication is important, and quite different from managing every teensy detail of a job.

The other problem with constantly controlling is that, like fear, it wears you out just as it wears out the people you're trying to control.

And what are you supposed to be doing if you're not meddling in other workers' jobs? You're keeping track of the big picture, of course. You are hitting your mark, improving the quality of your product or service, and growing in the job. That will keep you busy enough.

Political Skills: Thinking on Your Feet

With all the other skills you need to master, you don't hear a lot about thinking on your feet. That's because it is very hard to teach. If it were even possible to learn, your best bet would probably be to take a course in stand-up comedy or acting—not because your work is either comedy or acting, but because your work is, on many occasions, performance. And performing includes such skills as improvisation and the ability to think quickly and make decisions without the luxury of time for reflection.

You can prepare only so much for a presentation or a meeting. After that, you must be ready to respond to your boss and co-workers. You hope for applause, but more likely you'll get heckling, objections, or tough questions.

We think of work as what we do at our work stations. But how many times have you been stopped in the hall, the cafeteria, or the parking lot by someone who wanted to gossip, give you a tip, or ask a favor?

Information, opportunities, ideas: a lot of important business goes on far from the relative safety of your work station. Wherever it goes on, you have to be prepared to respond—not later in a memo, but right then and there.

Keep Your Head

Aside from such casual but important contacts, much of your work consists of how well you handle yourself in stressful situations for which you can't plan. If you can think on your feet, you can keep your head.

How do you do that? Here are a few techniques that will get you through: silence, neutrality, and honesty. These are all defensive tactics that give you time to think and react well. You also have to be able to make decisions on the spot, make judgments on people, and neutralize awkward situations. And when you need to go on the offense, it helps to be stubborn and determined in putting forward your ideas.

Silence   You've heard a lot about supportive listening, nodding, smiling, and encouraging the speaker. All of those are fine, but don't forget the value of plain old silence. Resist the temptation to fill a lull in a conversation. Be the one who sits quietly and lets others run their mouths. You will be amazed at how much you learn. Take in information, but don't commit yourself prematurely or impulsively. When in doubt, you are safest when you keep your mouth shut.

Neutrality   In so many situations, a co-worker will try to pressure you into a decision or a commitment. Or you may pressure yourself, feeling as if you must say *something*. Well, you don't have to commit yourself on the spot. If pressed, remain open and honest, but noncommittal. ("I really don't know enough about that to tell you what to do. I'll check into it and we can talk tomorrow.")

Honesty . . . But   You shouldn't lie to protect yourself. It's fine to react honestly: "That sounds like something I'd like to get involved with, but. . . ." The word *but* is your pivot. It allows you to express an honest reaction without committing you prematurely to someone else's project or idea. After "but," you can add the appropriate buffer, like ". . . but I need to finish my presentation before I commit to anything new."

Keep on Going

When you're the one promoting an idea, think of Donald Trump. Even if you can't stand him, you have to give the guy credit for the way he just keeps plowing through, making the points *he* wants to make. When the cameras and tape recorders are pointed at him, he makes use of the opportunity—for his purposes.

In a recent TV interview, he simply ignored any awkward questions from the interviewer. Instead, he made the points that were important to him. He dominated the conversation. He just kept talking.

People like Donald Trump don't get as far as they do by being shy, polite, or modest, or by doing what other people expect them to do. You don't have to act like him, but you can certainly be inspired by his persistence.

What we think of as virtues can be major liabilities when you're getting your carefully prepared presentation stuffed back down your throat by someone who's more aggressive. So, are you going to be shy, well-mannered, and modest, or are you going to make sure that your ideas prevail?

You don't have to do these things in a boorish way, but you must do them. Find a way that works for you. If someone is talking loudly, you can talk louder—or softer. If he's sitting, stand up to him—literally—and dominate with your physical presence. Find the techniques that work best for you—but it will be a lot easier if you are determined to dominate. Later, think back on how you handled yourself, and use any mistakes you made as lessons for the future.

One last reminder: notice that I said "thinking on your feet," not "talking on your feet." If you think first, you'll probably talk a lot less. And by mastering the impulse to fill space with talk, you'll already be well ahead in the politics game. You'll make fewer mistakes, and if you listen closely, you'll be amazed by how much you can learn.

If you still think of office politics as sleazy, it may help to re-name it "office anthropology." That makes you a researcher studying the tribe. The difference is, this is *your* tribe. And you are not some disinterested scientist. What you learn can protect your job and help you steer clear of bloody interoffice warfare. And if you forget every other political skill, remember this one: Listen more than you talk.

Chapter 7

Suffering from a Rotten Image

The Makeover

Most of us don't have the nerve or the freedom to job-
hop until we get the right job. Even with increased turnover, you
can still expect to see five years on a job go by like lightning. During those five years, you have plenty of time to dig yourself into a
very bad hole. People will label you as a loser, lazy, or unmoti-
vated, and you'll never know why. Nobody will ever tell you what
the problem is; some of them may not even know, they may just
have picked up bad vibes about you from others. You develop the
career equivalent of bad breath—but you will see the evidence.
You gradually become invisible.

Or you can use that same period of time to confront your bad
image and change it. If you stick with it, you can go from un-

touchable to A-list. Follow the advice in this chapter, and you can, with a little patience, reform even the funkiest bad image.

During your image makeover, time is on your side. The collective memory of a workplace is long, but it doesn't last forever. The people who think you stink will move up and out, and new people, who have no preconceived notions about you, move in. Meantime, you've been working hard on your image makeover and you'll be ready to shine.

Does This Story Sound Familiar?

A reader from Ohio wrote me that the rest of her team seemed to have forgotten about her:

> "(They) only see me as the receptionist. I have a lovely voice for the phone (at least once a week I'm told). I greet each employee and vendor with a warm smile every time. I wear well-groomed office clothes.
>
> "My team is getting training and moving around, and I'm at the front desk smiling day after day while my heart aches.
>
> "What should I do? I get along well with my co-workers. I get on committees to help out on programs. But I am left behind. Help!"

This worker's job description may be receptionist, but she suffers from a bad case of *secretary syndrome*. It's a common workplace image problem. People underestimate you, take you for granted, and overlook you.

Get Advice

Talk to someone (not your boss, not yet) who can be frank with you about your chances for advancement. This person should be someone who likes you and wants you to succeed. She should also be a realist who understands the political climate in your office and can guide you through it. But most important of all, this person should be someone who can tell you what is holding you back. This part may be painful for you, but it is vital to know. You can't get unstuck until you know what is keeping you stuck.

It may be some personal quality or skill that you need to work on. It may be that you need training. Whatever it is, you may be surprised or hurt by what you hear, but take it for what it is: an obstacle to overcome.

Your adviser can also give you realistic limits. For instance, she may tell you that you can advance by a stage or two, but no further. You don't have to settle for that judgment, but you should at least listen to a realistic assessment from someone who understands how your workplace operates.

Make a Plan

With help from your adviser, you can sketch a plan for advancement. Your next step is to present that plan to your boss and make the boss your ally in achieving it.

Expect resistance from your boss. It's much easier to leave people in the jobs they're in; developing employees takes much more time and energy. So your plan must include persuasion. You must show your boss exactly how you will be even more useful in a new position.

Declare Your Intentions

Tell your boss that you would like to position yourself for a better job. If you have done it before, it's time to do it again. Don't settle for vague promises and reassurances. You and your boss should work on a time frame and a series of steps for achieving your goal.

Image Control

As tough as it is to gain the skills to improve your position at work, it can be even tougher to change the image your team members have of you as a subordinate and not an equal partner.

Once you start to change, you also have to help others change their attitudes toward you. When you get to the point where your job responsibilities have grown, you may need to gently but firmly remind people that you are no longer the person who pulls jammed paper out of the copy machine. You can show them that instead, you are now the person who can help them do their jobs better by coaxing valuable information out of balky computers.

You are looking at a long process of educating others that you are different and that their relationship to you has changed. It may seem unfair: not only must you learn new skills, but you must also run your own personal image-changing campaign. You probably will feel that you already have enough new stresses without adding another one.

But image control is one of the most valuable lessons you can learn. In addition to doing the job, you must also be able to sell your way into the next one. And while you're at it, you can practice patience and diplomacy.

Changing your image is a slow and sometimes painful process. Occasionally it just doesn't work. If you find that you can't budge your subordinate image in your present team, then you should consider the alternative of moving to another department or company. This way you can start a different job, one more like what you want to be doing five years from now. But you can also start with a fresh image, one that you control from the beginning.

How to Be Viewed As a Grown-Up

Maybe your image is the life of the party—fun on Friday nights, but not the one to get the promotions. There's a connection, you know. See if this sounds familiar.

You know you do good work, but you always seem to get passed over for the really good jobs. Is there something about you that's telegraphing that you haven't got what it takes to handle more responsibility?

Check off any of the following statements that apply to you:

1. On Monday mornings, when people are standing around the copy machine talking about what happened Saturday night, I'm the one they're talking about: "Man, I couldn't be-lieeeeve it! Standing on top of the bar balancing a shot glass on his head!" □

2. At meetings, I'm always the one who makes the jokes. Sure, it's a little distracting, but it breaks up the boredom. □

3. Maybe I don't always get to work on time, but I get the job done (mostly). □

4. I enjoy talking with my co-workers about how much I drink and party. □

5. I say what I think, when and where I want to. □

6. I frequently start sentences with "I can't . . ." □

7. When the boss comes to me with an extra project, I can usually wiggle out of doing it. □

8. I love gossip and I can't keep a secret, even if I'm not 100 percent sure I have the facts straight. □

9. What I wear to work is my business. □

10. So what if people think I'm a little flaky? □

We're not talking about the quality of your work—we're talking about the reputation you have built for yourself. You may not realize it, but if several of the above statements apply to you, you may have saddled yourself with a reputation for being more interested in your social life than your work.

Once you get a reputation, it's a difficult thing to shake, particularly a bad one. Aside from your work, all your boss may know about you is the way you look and what you talk about—and what other people say about you. Put it this way: if you were the boss and that was all you had to go on, what would *you* conclude about you?

You may think that what you do on your own time is your own business. (And it is more likely to remain your own business if you also talk about it on your own time.) You may also think that people should not make judgments on you based on such "superficial" matters as your clothing, your jokes, or chance remarks. It may be your opinion that the trouble with bosses is that they need to lighten up and be a little more liberal in their thinking, especially when it comes to you.

You're entitled to all of those opinions. The problem is that "superficial" things are all part of the information you're communicating about yourself to your boss. While no individual element may be so bad, it can all add up to an overall negative impression of you.

The thing about most bosses is that they're conservative. They have to be, because they are held responsible by their bosses for getting results. When they're deciding who's going to get the important jobs, they want to assure themselves that they're picking someone they can trust with the responsibility—and someone who won't blab everything after the first beer on Friday night. All other things being equal, if one person projects an image of irresponsibility, who do you think the boss is going to eliminate first?

You don't have to change your personality in order to get ahead. You do have to realize that your boss and others can't help but make judgments about you based on those things that they see and hear.

If you feel you might have a reputation problem, you can tone it down, but it's going to take some time and patience on your part. You're going to have to think before you speak, modulate what you say, and gradually change your appearance and some of your habits. The alternative is to find another workplace where more people look and talk like you. But unless you hate your current job, it's going to take a lot less trouble to make small changes to fit in where you are now. You may worry that changing is selling out. In some people's eyes it probably is, but it certainly beats the alternative—selling yourself short.

Your Boss Is Watching You

Ever get the feeling that somebody's watching you? It's your boss. And your boss is making judgments about you based on those observations. If you're having image problems, it may be because the boss doesn't like what she sees.

Here are a few of the habits bosses watch for, along with ideas for making sure your boss likes what he sees. Let's start right at the beginning of your workday.

Lateness

Get to work on time. Seems so . . . second grade, doesn't it? But the fact is, the people who come in on time don't seem to mind the boss's fetish with promptness. The ones who hate being reminded to be prompt seem to be the same ones who often drag in late. Funniest thing, huh? And who do you think the boss will cut some slack for: the one who is chronically late, or the one who is chronically on time?

There are many causes of chronic lateness: disorganization, trying to do too much before work, and resentment. Solving the first two is a matter of thinking ahead (Do I have a clean shirt for tomorrow?) and acknowledging your limits (I really can't do three loads of laundry and make it to work on time).

Resentment is tougher, because you may not even want to own up to it. Maybe you don't like your boss or your job, so you come in late as a way of avoiding an unpleasant situation. It may be more awkward in the short run, but you need to face that problem and resolve it. When you begin to enjoy work again, you'll make it there on time.

Unprofessional Behavior

After you arrive at work, how long do you stand around talking about your weekend, reading the sports section, checking your E-mail, and telling jokes to your friends on the phone? A little socializing at work is a lubricant. A lot of socializing at work is called unprofessional. If you're not sure how much is too much, it's a good bet you should cut back.

Excuses

"Nobody told me . . ." "I didn't know . . ." "They didn't call me back . . ." "I thought Jack was doing that . . ." "You didn't tell me . . ." All of these excuses tell the boss that you were not planning, not anticipating problems, not asking the right questions, not taking responsibility for the details of a task you were given. Then, when you failed to produce work that was expected of you, you chose to blame someone else.

If you think about it, shifting the blame for not doing your job onto somebody else seems so . . . second grade, doesn't it? And shifting the blame to your boss is just dumb.

Caught? Apologize and accept the blame. Don't start thinking up excuses to fill that scary silence coming from your boss.

Your boss will be watching you even more after you make a mistake. This is your chance to win back some of the trust you have lost. That means doing your job better than ever. It's also a good time to do something extra or volunteer for a task. That's how you signal that you're back on track.

Poor Communication

Some people resent having to tell the boss where they are going or what they are doing. But, as with getting to work on time, the people who communicate well with their bosses don't mind having to do it.

You also have a responsibility to communicate problems. You're not allowed to sulk and tell everybody that the boss dumped on you. First, you have to give the boss a chance to help you resolve the problem. Think of communication as an ongoing dialogue with your boss. Some days you're in conflict, others you're in sync. And over the long term, you build trust and mutual respect.

If your boss seems to be checking on you a lot, that means you're making her ask you when you should be volunteering information about what you are doing. Communication is a wonderful way to soothe the micromanager.

Saying No

You can get in very big trouble for saying no—it's called insubordination when you do it blatantly enough to get fired. So we develop ways to say no that never use the word. Some people just ignore orders. Others say they will do something, then never do it. Or they put off a task for so long that someone else does it. If it's part of your job, do it. Remember, however, that you are allowed to say no to an order that is unethical or dangerous.

Are You Dependable?

Are you marveling at how second-grade basic this advice is? Instead, marvel at how many people ignore it. And, funniest thing, they're often the same ones who wonder why their bosses nag them so much.

How to Take the Initiative

One of the qualities that separates passive, expendable employees from vital, indispensable leaders is initiative—the ability to plan, act, and think your way through a situation.

The key to initiative is self-motivation, being confident and willing enough to solve problems on your own without waiting for someone to tell you what to do. One of the reasons why initiative is so valuable is that so few people seem to have any. Here are some ways you can cultivate initiative in yourself:

Initiative Is . . .

- Behaving like a low-maintenance worker. Why do you think bosses are so fond of workers who show initiative? Because they don't have to spend their valuable time telling them what to do, and then reminding them every day.
- Previsualizing situations, imagining the obstacles—and how you are going to solve them.
- Asking yourself the questions—and answering them—before you ask your supervisor. If you get in the habit of solving problems on your own, you are developing one of the basic skills of initiative.
- Taking responsibility for more than just your little box.
- Making mental connections. Cultivate an understanding of how the total organization works, where your job fits in. Knowing the connections will help you do a more thorough job.
- Making connections with people. Forming cooperative relationships will benefit you in almost any work-related project. People with initiative recognize how working with the strengths of others can only increase their own strength and that of the entire work group.
- Being thorough. Some people show partial initiative by coming up with an idea, but they lose interest or don't have suffi-

cient skill to fill in the blanks and complete the less glamorous step-by-step details. Initiative is more than just starting something—it means finishing it too.

- Being persistent. Someone is always going to say no to you. Your job is to figure out how to turn them around or get around them.
- Thinking in a creative way. When other people are saying, "But we always do it this way," you are saying, "What's a better way to do it?"
- An invitation to your boss to notice your work and promote you. When managers look for people to add to their teams, they look for people who deliver.

Initiative Is Not . . .

- Waiting for someone to tell you what to do.
- Excusing your mistakes by saying something like, "But I didn't understand." When you have struggled to understand, but still don't, that's when you must open your mouth and ask a question.
- Marching off on your own without including anyone else in your plans. This is not initiative; it is the formula for disaster. In a business situation—or any other situation, for that matter—you owe it to the people involved to share your ideas with them.

  The people who are most likely to understand how much they need others are those who work alone. Freelancers, the successful ones at least, quickly develop a professional support system that includes people with whom they can trade favors, ideas, encouragement, and information.

  But, you may protest, doesn't that mean they lack initiative? Nope. It means they are smart enough to know their limitations, realize the value of collaborating with others, and seek help when they need it.
- Crushing everyone in your path. Don't confuse aggression or pig-headedness with initiative.

- Assuming. Does this sound familiar? Right after any major snafu, one or more people can be counted on to protest, "But I assumed you were going to do that!" Workers with initiative assume nothing and double-check everything. It's not that they don't trust others. It's more that they take an interest in the whole process, not just their part of it.

Getting the Edge

The edge: Do you have it? What is it?

People who have the edge share a number of characteristics. They are successful, but never at the expense of others. They are long-term survivors in the business world, which has a way of devouring its own. They survive because they maintain friends and inspire loyalty. They keep their friends because they are loyal to them. These friends invariably describe them, in glowing terms, as people they can count on for anything.

Here are some of the qualities that can help you develop the edge:

- *Dependability.* Do what you say you will do. This can be tricky, because it involves a certain amount of self-knowledge and self-management. If you say you'll turn in a piece of work at 9 A.M. on Friday, you have to know how long it will take you to finish it. Never say, "I can't" before you've tried.
- *Trustworthiness.* You may hear gossip, but you don't have to pass it along. Keep secrets. If you get a reputation for discretion, everyone will confide in you and you'll know everything that's going on, even if you don't talk about it.
- *Responsibility.* People with the edge accept responsibility for their actions. They don't brag when they succeed and they don't blame when they fail. They freely give credit to their associates. They apologize when they're wrong.
- *Communication.* Call people back. Write short, friendly notes to stay in touch. Keep in touch with your network of friends and associates.

- *Generosity.* Make a habit of generosity. Do things for free. Volunteer. Give away favors, small bits of advice, job tips. All that good will come back to you.

Look for opportunities to put people in touch with each other. If you recommend a friend for a job, you've given that friend a tremendous compliment and you have earned some long-term loyalty.

Even though you sometimes must say no to a request, you must always seem to be saying yes. Here's one way to do it: Whenever you decide you can't do something, give a credible reason and then offer to help in some other way. ("I can't manage this project for you because I'm right in the middle of this assignment for my boss, but I'd be willing to spend an hour going over it with you.")

- *Courtesy and kindness.* Speak well of people, or don't speak at all. This includes people who have fired you, wronged you, and spoken badly about you. (Nobody said getting the edge would be easy.)

Don't fall into the self-indulgent and destructive habit of nursing grudges, and discourage others who do. If you always answer such people with a positive comeback—or at least a noncommittal smile—they will soon enough tire of confiding their gripes to you.

Display good manners at all times, particularly to those who actively antagonize you. It will drive them absolutely crazy. It may also win them over.

- *Ethics.* Develop a standard of behavior you can live with. That means that when you make tough decisions, you feel you've done the right thing, even if it hurts.

Sometimes you'll need the courage to disagree with the prevailing beliefs. If you feel someone is going down a wrong path, you'll have to say so, even if it means risking a friendship.

- *Perspective.* Develop a sense of humor and humility about what happens to you. No matter how grim the experience, give yourself a boost by figuring out a way to make yourself smile about it. Or if you can't get over it any other way, you can borrow my shortcut to perspective: we're all made of about 80 percent water, so that means all our problems are 80 percent water too. Think about that.

• *Industriousness.* Find a reason to do your job well—if not for your own satisfaction, at least for the pleasure of doing something, anything, right.

• *Persistence.* Almost anyone has one good idea, one good effort, one good impulse. The people with the edge prove themselves by repeating their best performances year after year.

If this is all beginning to sound like excerpts from the Boy Scout manual, you're right. How many of us memorized these words: "A scout is trustworthy, loyal, helpful, friendly, courteous, kind, obedient, cheerful, thrifty, brave, clean, and reverent"? How many of us could chart our course through adulthood by the times we defaulted on those virtues?

It is lifetime values like those that guide people with the edge through long and successful careers. Corny? Perhaps. But consider David Brown. The successful producer of *Cocoon, Jaws,* and *The Sting* ought to have left a trail of enemies all the way from California to New York, right? On the contrary. The writer of a recent article in *Vanity Fair* couldn't find a soul to speak badly of Brown. In fact, his associates described him as someone with old-fashioned virtues, always speaking well of others and sending thank-you notes at the drop of his stylish hat. The article concluded that Brown is likely to be successful in launching a new production company, because he has built "an army of well-wishers."

You don't get the edge overnight. It takes time to get that sharp. So you might as well start now. In business, you're only as good as your relationships.

The Parable of the Sink Strainer

If you want to understand how people respond to problems, just sit quietly in a corner of the employee breakroom and watch.

In the breakroom is a sink, used mostly for cleaning out plastic food containers. During lunchtime, people rinse out remnants of their meals—perhaps spaghetti, chicken, or tuna salad. Soon, the sink strainer fills up with an unsavory soup, made of all these bits of lunches. Then, from your corner, you will begin to hear comments like these:

- Eeeeeee-yuw! That's disgusting!
- Can you believe that people would leave a mess like that?
- Somebody ought to do something about this!

Some of these people are continuing to dump junk into the strainer while making these comments. They just don't get it. Meanwhile, the sink strainer gets fuller, until water won't drain through it and the funky bits of food overflow into the sink itself. Left long enough, the drain will clog.

(Let's pause in this drama for a moment, to let you pick which of the above reactions sounds most like you. We'll discuss those answers in a minute.)

Now, if you wait just a little longer, you may be in for a surprise. Along comes someone who rinses a container into the sink strainer and then—amazing!—empties the sink strainer into the nearest garbage can.

Maybe where you work, it's not a sink strainer, it's a microwave crusted with spills nobody wiped up. Whatever the problem, the way people react to it is an indication of how they react to workplace problems in general.

A sink strainer or a messy microwave or a quota that just doesn't get met, they're all problems. Even though everyone may share equally in causing the problem, people have a way of distancing themselves from the responsibility of solving it. It's almost as if they thought there were some Department of Problem Solving whose job is to clean up other people's messes. (Want to locate that department? Here's how: if your building has 14 floors, that department can be found on the 15th floor.)

Then there are those workers who just go ahead and take responsibility, without assigning blame. Such people do more than their job descriptions. You wouldn't hear them say, "Oh, I'll clean out my own stuff from this sink strainer, but I'm leaving those two green beans. I didn't put them there, so they're not my department."

Maybe you did not see yourself in any of the responses. Maybe you wanted to fill in another answer, because you realized that someone had to take action, and that someone was you. If so, that responsible worker may be you.

If you're looking for a definition of responsibility, here it is: If something happens at work, and if it affects you, it *is* your problem. That is not to say that you have to make a career out of taking on problems that other people ignore. You'd soon burn out if you tried. But you can still act or speak up or recruit others to help you solve those problems. In other words, you can do your part.

If you prefer, you can look at problems in a more pragmatic way: it's easier, less time consuming, and less annoying to take care of a small problem than to try to fix it when it turns into a big problem.

So, where do you start? You can start as the Angel of the Sink Strainer did, by being a good example for others. By taking responsibility for a little extra work, you are also taking a modest ethical stand, showing others that this is "the way we do things around here." Granted, that method takes a lot of patience, not to mention faith in human nature.

In addition, you can speak up. The next time someone is moaning about a problem and waiting for someone from that mythical Department of Problem Solving to appear magically and take care of things, speak up: "I have an idea. How about if we . . ." And then recruit the complainer into action.

While you have the complainer's attention, ask for suggestions about how to solve this problem. Both of you may be surprised how many good ideas the complainer has. Then each of you can recruit someone else, and so on, until you have an action team. Before long, you'll all be saying, "No problem!"

The great thing about an image makeover is that it allows you to survive some of your past mistakes and indiscretions. Yes, like Madonna, you can reinvent yourself. You will need to take a look at your past behavior—a painful task—and change those habits that have branded you a loser. You could hop to another job to avoid the image makeover, but guess what? Your bad habits tag along wherever you go, and it's only a matter of time before they start to undermine you again.

Chapter 8

Succumbing to Stress and Burnout

Burnouts are a lot like two-pack-a-day smokers: they have absolutely convinced themselves that they are just fine, thank you. And the insomnia, the fatigue, the divorce, the drinking, the high blood pressure? Nothing to do with being burned out, thank you very much.

In short, burnouts have gotten to the point where they don't pay attention to their own bodies, and probably not to people who care about them either. So the first step to overcoming your own burnout is to take a quick look at yourself and what's going on around you. Why even bother, if you're already in a state of denial? Because stress kills, burnout kills—sometimes in dramatic ways, like the massive heart attack; sometimes in slower ways, like alcoholism and chronic depression. And it is sure to kill your enjoyment, enthusiasm, and joy in what you do and the people you love.

You owe it to yourself to guard your own health and safety while at work. Here are some things you can do to protect your health on the job.

Educate Yourself

Ignorance will not protect you from illness. Knowing the risks is an important part of maintaining your safety and health on the job.

You should know the common occupational risks of your job. If workers in your field are developing back injuries, certain cancers, headaches, or eyestrain, or are suffering a higher-than-normal rate of miscarriage, you should be aware of these facts in order to protect yourself.

Work- and stress-related behavioral disorders are less obvious, but just as lethal. Is your profession one of those with a higher rate of substance abuse, alcoholism, divorce, and depression? Is it a young person's profession, where people work hard and long, and then get out because they can't stand the pace anymore?

You can get more specific information about job-related illnesses from your human resource development office; your union; trade publications in your industry; and newspapers and television, which report trends in worker health and safety.

Look Around You

This is my absolute favorite way of getting perspective on your workplace. (It's also a good way to check out a place where you think you might like to work.)

The people with whom you work can be a mirror of your own

physical and mental health, now and in the future. Look at their eyes, their posture, their skin. Listen to what they say, how they talk about their work. What do they complain about? What makes them happy? If you observe closely, you may notice that a number of people are having trouble sleeping, popping aspirin or antacids all the time, or frequently saying, "I hate my job." You should take this as a warning, particularly if they are in the majority.

Look hardest at the old-timers and the lifers—people who have been in your business for 10 years or more. Ten years from now, would you like to look like, or sound like, or be in the same physical condition as these people? If not, there are changes you can make now in your work habits and lifestyle that can protect you in the future and help you have a long and satisfying career.

Observe yourself, too. How do you sit or stand while doing your job? What thoughts and worries are running through your mind as you work? How do you feel when you walk in on Monday morning? How do you feel when you leave? You can begin to combat burnout when you make yourself aware of its creeping up on you.

Use It

When your company offers you safety equipment—helmets, safety glasses, telephone headsets, earplugs, glare screens, back braces—use it. The nuisance of using this equipment is small compared to the risk of developing hearing loss, repetitive stress injuries, or other ailments that could impair your ability to work.

Observe the Basics

Learn how to lift, bend, and stretch properly. Use the right tools and keep them close by so you won't strain yourself reaching for them. Keep your work area clean, orderly, and free of hazards.

Read the safety instructions on the chemicals and substances you use. Is your equipment in good working order, and properly aligned for your body?

Take a Break

Particularly if your job keeps you in one position, you should get up and move around for five minutes at least once an hour. Most of your day you may spend trying to increase your concentration; in this case, the object is to break your concentration. Intense concentration, worry, and stress may cause you to hold your body in unnatural postures. Take notice of where your body hurts and loosen up.

Running Hot and Cold

If you work outside, you are vulnerable to extremes of heat and cold and exposure to sun and wind. Dress appropriately for the weather. Protect yourself from prolonged exposure to the sun with protective clothing, headgear, and sunblock.

Workers who must be outside in subfreezing temperatures buddy up with co-workers and observe each other for early symptoms of frostbite. They also take frequent breaks in a warm or sheltered area.

Even if you don't work under extreme conditions, it's a good idea for you and a co-worker to buddy up on health and safety issues. The two of you can research job hazards in your field and learn to protect each other from them.

Not Just at Work

Regular moderate physical exercise can benefit you by loosening up those muscles that get cramped at work. You also can loosen up your stressed-out mind by walking, running, swimming, or bicycling off some of the tension you built up during the workday. Ask your doctor to clear you for a program of exercise.

How Do You Manage Stress?

Do you manage stress in unhealthy ways, such as smoking; overeating, eating poorly, or skipping meals; using painkillers, tranquilizers, or sleeping pills; or drinking too much? Exercise can also be helpful for people trying to control or quit those bad habits. Start substituting healthy stressbusters for the unhealthy ones.

While I was still a smoker, I started swimming every morning. At the beginning, I was lighting up right after swimming a half-mile. After a while, smoking started getting in the way of swimming. It still took me a long time to break the habit, but swimming helped me change my image of myself, and that was part of the battle.

The Myth of Having It All

It's convenient to think of stress and burnout as coming from the outside. Some of it does. As life goes on, you develop more responsibilities, people expect more of you, and your life really does get busier. That's not a myth. That's reality.

But there is much more to stress than that. In fact, I don't even want you to worry about externally imposed stress until you have looked at how you add stress to your own life through buying into the myth of Having It All.

In recent memory, this myth goes back to that TV commercial where the woman sings, "I can bring home the bacon, fry it up in a pan, and never let you forget you're a man, 'cause I'm a woman . . ." It seemed doable at the time, so we kept working long hours even after we had children, and took on more financial responsibilities—a bigger house, a new car, more expensive vacations.

Finally, one day you wake up to realize that every moment of your life has been scheduled. You're tired all the time. The "all" in having it all is crushing you. You enjoy little or nothing of "all" that you have.

You need to stop right now and decide which of the excess baggage you can jettison.

OK, all you burnout cases, we're going to have to be brutally frank. Are you doing it all because you have to, or because you choose to? And if you choose to, are you really choosing, or just refusing to choose? By that I mean, are you refusing to choose to be a person who can only do so much? Are you refusing to choose because you're hanging on to an impossible image of yourself—and sacrificing your sanity for it?

Let me elaborate. We all have an image of ourselves. And an image, I hasten to say up front, is an illusion. It is cobbled together from what our parents told us, what our school friends told us, and ideas we got from watching TV commercials in our impressionable years.

Kiss Me, You Fool

Let me give you an example: lipstick. If you look at magazines and TV commercials, you get the impression that lipstick must always be worn and must always be perfectly applied. Since in ads they only show lipstick on beautiful young women, the image (illusion!) is that you, too, will be beautiful and desirable to men if you wear lipstick.

Anyone who does wear lipstick knows it takes almost constant maintenance to get that perfect look. And guess what? I've never met a man who actively wanted to kiss lips covered with greasy petroleum by-products, which is what lipstick is when you remove its image. So much for that illusion.

You'll have to fill in the blanks on what your own image is, but just for the sake of discussion, let's make one up. See if it sounds familiar: You must be physically attractive; you must be successful; if you have a family, it must be happy and fulfilling for all. And your children must be physically attractive and successful. . . .

Are you beginning to see that you could chase your image all your life and never achieve it? Meanwhile, living in tandem with your image is your real life. In it, you are presentable-looking (most days), you have a pretty good job, and your family gets along pretty well.

You can see that the stress, and eventually burnout, comes in when you concentrate on achieving your image—which, remember, is something in your head—and don't give yourself credit for what you accomplish in your real life. If you believe in your image, but you don't live up to it (and who does?) you will rate yourself low.

That means even your real-life accomplishments will be tarnished; you will discount them because they don't match your image. If you keep striving for something that always eludes you, you will be miserable—and stressed out.

No More Radish Rosettes

On the other hand, what would happen if you started choosing based on your real life? Once again, you will have to fill in the blanks with your own circumstances, but here's a hypothetical situation: "I am a working parent and I choose to go to bed at 10 P.M. tonight rather than cutting radishes into little rosettes for the vegetable platter I am making for the party." Don't forget the really important choice: "And furthermore, I will not apologize, to myself or anyone else, because there are no radish rosettes." (Maybe it isn't radish rosettes, but I bet you can think of something equally wacky that you chose to do—probably in the middle of the night—to live up to some image.)

How to Do It

Every time you're stressed, you must make a choice. Ask yourself, "Who am I really, and what's really important to me?" Then make your choice. The best way to dismantle your image is piece by piece, radish by radish, choice by choice. It will help if you concentrate on the absurdity of some of your past fiascoes and vow never to get in such situations again.

Choosing means you have to give up your image. If you refuse to choose, you can only conclude that your image is more important to you than your sanity.

Central to all of this is that you have to be doing something that is important to you, only you, and not your image, which is never satisfied anyway. That one important something is like the diamond in your necklace—it energizes you. After that, everything else will fall into place.

The Eeyore Syndrome (Something Bad Always Happens to Me)

Many people deal with setbacks by complaining about their bad luck—much like A. A. Milne's perennially depressed donkey, Eeyore. I imagine this sounds very familiar. The problem is, if you habitually deal with setbacks (large or small) by feeling sorry for yourself or accepting them fatalistically, you're eroding your confidence and energy. Confidence and energy are stressbusters that you need to activate, not undermine.

We're already aware of the external problems that contribute to stress: too much work, conflicts with co-workers, family troubles, paying the bills. We also know that most of us have negative mental habits that can kick in during stressful times and make a bad situation even worse. But what are those habits? How can we identify them? And, most important, how can we control them?

The worst thing about negative mental messages is that they're sneaky; most of the time you may not be aware that you're dragging yourself down. The first step is to bring these messages to the surface. So here's an exercise to try.

"Why Me?"

The next time you're stuck in a line of cars waiting for an endless freight train to go by, or when it's been four red lights and you still haven't made that left turn, listen to what you're saying to yourself:

- Why does this have to happen when I'm already late?
- This *always* happens.
- Why me?
- This is what I get for not leaving on time.
- If only I had . . .

You can go on and on like this until traffic starts moving again, listening to your internal dialogue and making note of how you are blaming yourself, blaming others, blaming the fates, and generally giving yourself a lot of unnecessary grief about something that is probably nothing but a random occurrence. You're fuming, you're picking on yourself. And all for a freight train.

Once you've picked up on this negative wavelength, you will have an easier time noticing it when it turns up again, as it probably will, at the worst possible times in your life.

Let's say you're working on a project that is very hard for you. In addition to the mental effort of just doing the job itself, you are probably sending yourself negative failure messages that intrude on your concentration and make a hard job just that much more difficult: "I should have figured that out the first time . . ." "I'm just stupid . . ." "Everybody is laughing at me . . ." "Why am I so slow at this? . . ." "If I screw this up, I'll never get another shot. . . ." And on and on. With that kind of negative cheerleading going on in your head, it's a wonder you don't just give up, or make even more mistakes.

Challenge the Message

Each of those messages is a shorthand form of some larger way you may be running yourself down: perfectionism, inflexibility, pessimism, unrealistic expectations, self-consciousness, feeling like a perpetual victim. You can't change them all at once, but you can see them for what they are: needlessly self-destructive.

Once you realize how much you're harassing yourself and possibly even setting yourself up to fail, it's time to start challenging those negative signals. Since you're trying to break a bad habit, you will need a lot of patience and vigilance—and you will need to make an effort to forgive yourself for the mistakes you do make.

Replace It

Start replacing each negative mental message with a positive one. Depending on how set in your ways you are, you may need to use logic, humor, inspirational sayings—or all of the above, in different situations. As an exercise, you can even take your negativism to absurd new heights: "Look on the bright side. Maybe if I hadn't gotten stuck waiting for that freight train, I would have gotten hit by a bus running a red light at the next intersection. So it's actually good that it happened." Use any or all techniques that will break the spell of negativism. But make a resolution that you won't continue undermining yourself with what is nothing more than a very cruel form of self-torture.

Much of what happens to us is just an occurrence. We get into trouble as soon as we start to make an occurrence mean more than it needs to. You get stuck in traffic; you get a new boss; you struggle with a tough job: these are all facts. You can use them to run yourself down, or you can see them for what they are, and move on.

The Cure: Getting Control of Your Impulse to Control

If you're suffering job stress, one of the most important elements to examine is control. Who's got it? Can you take some of it? Are you controlling the right things or the wrong things in your life? Can you let go of it?

Out of Control

One of the symptoms of stress is feeling out of control: the demands of other people (boss, spouse, family) seem to be controlling your life. There seems to be no space in your life that isn't controlled, except maybe sleep, and that may be controlled by nightmares about work.

Who's Got Control?

You may describe your stressed-out life in terms such as these: "My boss expects me to . . ." or "In order to keep my job I have to. . . ." Such statements only fuel your panicky feeling of being controlled by others. You may remember having the same feeling in college after five teachers all gave you assignments due on the same day.

Face it: you can't possibly do all that is expected of you by other people. But as an adult, you can take control in ways you may not have known as a student: reschedule, delegate, abbreviate, set and meet realistic deadlines.

Some of the demands are in fact real, and you should make note of them, as well as how much time they take and when they need to be done. You can start to control inflexible demands by using the basic tools mentioned above: reschedule, delegate, abbreviate, set and meet realistic deadlines.

Your list of required tasks may be depressingly long, but you can control it by culling out the tasks that can be postponed, delegated, or abbreviated.

The Guilt List

But you must also identify self-imposed or perfectionist demands and put them on a second list, "Things I Should Be Doing." Some items on this list are important, but because you are not implementing them, they have turned into little nagging voices that you ignore and then feel bad about.

Do not discount, avoid, or postpone any item that involves a positive life change. If you let life goals slip away from you, you will be losing a most vital tool of control, and with it your ability to change your life.

Instead, you should make it a habit to take specific short-term steps toward any goal—like retraining, relocating, or getting a better job—that will improve your life in the long run.

Other items on this list, such as exercise and recreation, should be incorporated into your schedule. They will add to your general sense of well-being, which is also an important part of feeling in control.

What's left on your guilt list? Only the guilty baggage you carry around with you, which should be viewed as expendable. Everybody has a different guilt list, but you can spot guilt items because they are vague, impossible to accomplish, and never seem to get done.

Take Control

Your guilt list should now contain only nonessential demands you make on yourself. Think about it: you made all of those demands, so you can unmake them. Use whatever technique works best for you. You may want to make each item seem as absurd as possible by taking it to the limit. For example, if you like to work with sharp pencils, imagine sharpening all of the pencils in your office, then all of the pencils in the world, then starting all over on your pencils that are now dull. Or you can carry your guilt list around, take it out while you're waiting in line somewhere, and just laugh at it. Dream up a sitcom based on a person who does everything on that list. Or just toss the guilt list in the wastebasket. Say to yourself, "I will not be controlled by things I can't control."

"Lose" Control

When there is too much to do and too little time to do it, your life gets very regimented. So even when you start to take more control, you may feel as if even fun is just another item on a list: "Party, 9 P.M."

The only cure for this is to do something a little bit crazy. Don't sabotage your life by spending a weekend you can't afford gambling in Las Vegas; don't plan on arriving late for an important meeting. You want to do things to break up your routine just a little bit. Just this once, skip flossing your teeth the second time and use the extra time to take the scenic route to work. Pick your own harmless method of losing control. By surrendering control now and then, you can reinforce your overall sense of being in control.

How to Say No

Are you spread too thin? Here are some symptoms. You decide if they sound unpleasantly familiar:

- You have it all—and it's about to kill you.
- Everyone admires how much you accomplish—everyone but you.
- You do a lot, but you never seem to get anything done.
- As much as you accomplish, you feel like you're just drifting.
- When others ask for your help, you never say no.
- You feel like you are a good person only when you're doing something.
- You don't enjoy your life as much as you thought you would.

What's wrong with being spread too thin? It's that nagging feeling of being driven, but never being in the driver's seat. It's accomplishment without satisfaction. It's achieving other people's goals, not your own.

Let's say you decide to cut back on your activity level. Where would you begin? You can resolve not to volunteer for any new jobs for a month, until you can sort out what's most important among your activities. If you're spread too thin, you'll find it almost impossible not to volunteer. Alarms will be going off in your head, and they may sound like this: "But they can't do it without me!" In that case, you're falling for the old myth of indispensability. It's fine to feel wanted, but if you need to feel wanted in order to feel important, you're in trouble. Or how about, "They won't do it right without me" or "I might as well do it, because if I let someone else do it, I'll just have to do it all over again anyway." Such statements are variations on the myth of indispensability. Taken to its extreme, this attitude denies others—bosses, co-workers, family members—the important right to figure out things for themselves, make their own mistakes, and solve problems.

It also suggests that you're not a happy camper unless you've got control. Control, in itself, is a fine thing. Needing to have control all the time can be a problem. Doing other people's work for them or supervising too closely can make them overly dependent on you, which has a negative effect on their long-term productivity and growth as workers. Then, when you finally do take a day off, sure enough, things aren't done to your standards. When you return, you get the temporary satisfaction of saying, "See, they can't do it without me." But you have misunderstood your function. It's not to do everything; it's to do your part well and make it possible for others to do their part well too.

If you can keep yourself from automatically volunteering, at least for that one month, you will have made great progress toward decreasing your activity level. But you must also be ready to say no when others ask you. This will be nearly impossible if your self-image is based on what others think of you.

As with the need to control, depending on other people's opinion of you becomes a problem when it affects your behavior. If you say yes because you're afraid of what someone will think of you if you say no, you're in trouble.

If the test period goes well, you may find yourself with some blank spots on your calendar. You can use that freed-up time to think about big questions. If that's an unfamiliar feeling, all the more need to stop and do it. And if you feel a little panicky when you're not busy every waking hour, that's a sign that you may be putting off something important.

So, what are the big questions? "What do I want to accomplish with my job and my life?" "What does all this activity add up to?" "How much of what I do is for myself, not just for what somebody told me I was supposed to be?" "Am I happy?" Those are tough questions to answer. You can see how much easier it is to get on just one more task force or add just one more job to your list than to answer them bluntly.

The purpose of all this effort is not to make you selfish, just self-directed. Learning to say no to unnecessary activity will be easier once you resolve that you belong to yourself and not to others.

In the long run, your accomplishments and your commitment to others don't have to diminish, but they may change direction.

Instead of cleaning up after your family, for instance, you may teach them to clean up after themselves. Or, instead of feeling guilty because you don't bake cookies for them, you can teach them to bake cookies.

You can employ the same principles at work. If everyone in the office depends on you to solve their computer problems, you teach them how to solve their own—and make yourself less available each time they ask: "Remember, I showed you how to change the default."

If you feel like a heel for cutting loose people who depend on you, remind yourself that you are doing them a favor by teaching them to be more self-sufficient. And, of course, you are freeing yourself from a major source of stress and burnout.

Once you realize that stress and burnout, like the common cold, are going to creep up on you from time to time, you're better prepared to combat them. If your work is suffering, if your morale is bad, the first question to ask yourself is, "Have I allowed myself to get burned out?" Your best defense is to remind yourself of your priorities and make sure you say no to anything that distracts you from what you most need to do.

Chapter 9

Stagnating

Brain Death = Career Death

It's very difficult to tell where you are in your career. You spend most of your time just doing your job. You might not even ask yourself if you are happy or sad, or if there is anything more you can do.

But you do recognize that feeling of being stuck. Depending on your personal metabolism, you may get that feeling only once or twice in a career, or you may get it every couple of years. Part of having a long, successful work life is learning to recognize stagnation and master it.

Mastering the Long View

Are you getting too old for your job? I'm not talking about age. We all have the mental and physical potential to work many years past the traditional age of retirement. But you can be thirtysomething—or even younger—and still be an outdated old fogy if you're not knowledgeable about your job, your company, and your industry.

It's no longer sufficient just to know how to do your job. Working in these times when information and technology are accelerating, you can wake up suddenly to find yourself lagging behind others in your field. If you don't understand where your job fits into the big picture of your industry, you may be surprised to find that your job is about to disappear. That's guaranteed to make you feel very, very old.

You don't have to be a rocket scientist to bring yourself up to speed. You don't even need to stay up all night studying trends, charts, and graphs. You do have to put in a certain amount of regular effort, however.

Do you ever think any big-picture thoughts about your job— what it means, what it's worth, where it fits in your company and in your industry? You should always be trying to see where you and your job fit in the big picture. Here's an easy exercise to get you into the habit.

Whatever you read, hear, or see, focus the information by asking yourself, "How could this affect me? How can I take advantage of this news?" You'll be amazed how many news items, trends, and technological developments potentially affect you. In other cases, you'll just be interested in something you read or hear, but there won't be any apparent connection to what you do. That's when you have to be creative and say to yourself, "If this interests me, there must be some way I can connect it to what I do." This way of thinking might be foreign to you, but keep it up and eventually it will become habitual.

You must also learn to work defensively. In the old days, you might have been able to get away with keeping your head down and ignoring what's going on around you. But in this age of constant change, that's downright dangerous. If you're about to be replaced by computerized machinery, you don't want to be the last to find out. You want to be picking out your next job well in advance of that announcement.

Work offensively. These days, workers seldom stay in the same job for 25 or 30 years and bow out with a gold watch. You are likely to change companies, locations, and job descriptions several times in your career. Every time you make a change, you will be wise to study up on how your organization works. Knowing the unofficial working structure—who gets things done, who really has power, who's buddies with whom—can save you years of frustration.

Develop a Nose for News

Do you have any idea what's going on in your industry? If you don't, start finding out today. Fortunately, business trends take years to develop, so even if you've been asleep at the switch for years, you can still catch up. If there is a major change occurring in your field, experts have probably been analyzing it, predicting it, and dissecting it for a long time. Knowing what they are saying gives you time to regroup, retrain, or move on to a completely different field.

Get in the habit of scanning the *Wall Street Journal*, national weekly news magazines, and the major trade journals of your industry. Don't just read haphazardly. Look for news about technological developments, hiring trends, and other information that can affect your job. Is your industry expanding or shrinking? You should know.

If you are a buyer for a chain of clothing stores, for example, you need to keep track of the current upheavals in the retailing industry. Your company might be bought out next year. It might be going bankrupt. If you know that now, you can protect your job—or change it.

Once a week, scan your TV program guide for documentary programs on science or the future. Learn something about what's happening to the world, because it's happening to you too.

Read one recent book about your field.

Overcoming the Ostrich Factor

Get out of the know-nothing habit; get into the habit of asking tough questions. After you've been reading business news for a while, you'll be aware of worldwide turbulence and radical changes in virtually every industry. There is every reason to think the same could happen in your industry.

If you work for a bank, how will mergers in your industry affect your company? They could result in layoffs or reassignments. How will computers, online banking, and other technological changes affect service? If banking has been slow to promote women, should you take your skills to another field? Is your company financially sound? Buy a share or two of stock and study the annual report.

I Heard It Through the Grapevine

Are you a member of a professional association in your industry? For the price of an annual membership fee (which your company might pay) you can plug into a job hotline, speakers bureau, and sounding board for your colleagues, not to mention a ready-made grapevine that can answer just about any question you have.

Attend meetings of your professional association, and listen to what your colleagues are saying. Is the mood optimistic or desperate? Are there plenty of jobs to be had? Where are people moving to find work?

Pick out the people who seem most knowledgeable, and stay in touch with them. They can be terrific sources of information, advice, and job leads. As you become more knowledgeable, you can return the favor.

To Your Good Health

Do you look like an old-timer? Without becoming obsessed with your appearance, you should certainly become aware of where it puts you on the fogy spectrum.

Some people are so paranoid about appearing older than their colleagues that they are galloping to plastic surgeons for nips and tucks. You may not share such extreme feelings about your appearance, but there is still a great psychological advantage to looking and feeling youthful at work.

Regular, moderate exercise can hold off creaks and pains for years. It might keep your brain ticking a little faster, too.

If you are overweight, gradual, sensible weight loss will save you from the ailments that disable heavy people and the prejudices co-workers may feel toward you.

Get Busy

Now that you know what's going on, what are you going to do about it? It's time to develop a personal plan of action. Do you need retraining? Do you need more college? How much time do you have?

Even if your job is not in any immediate danger, it's a good idea to learn a new skill that will enhance your ability and make your job more interesting to you. That's what really keeps you young on the job.

Do You Have a Job or a Career?

If you've been stagnating for a while, you may not know the answer to this question. Here's how I distinguish job from career: A job is something you do to get food on the table. Skill and personal satisfaction are secondary to the need to make a living. Careers, on the other hand, are described in terms of commitment, control, and mastery. A career is distinguished from a job by continually increasing levels of personal and professional accomplishment by which you rate your progress. Careers usually pay better too, although some careers like teaching, preaching, or raising children seldom get paid what their service is truly worth.

But perhaps the most telling difference lies in the expression "dead-end job." You hardly ever hear of a "dead-end career." A dead-end job leads nowhere.

Not that a job must always become a career. Work is only one of many ways, along with family, friends, and service to others, to feel a sense of worth in this world. And all of us—yes, even the hotshots—have to balance job (economics) with satisfaction (career).

The other possibility is that you have been treating your perfectly good career like a job. With some fine-tuning of the way you look at your work, you can get back on a career track.

Look at it this way. Since you must work, you might as well ask yourself, "How good can I make this for myself?" That is the first step to turning a job into a career. Here are some of the factors you need to consider.

Commitment

This means continuing to work because it's important to you, makes you feel worthwhile, and gives you a sense of accomplishment or service. Commitment is something you have to bring to your work. Without commitment, you feel like a robot. With it, you're on your way to a career.

If you won big in the lottery tomorrow, could you walk away from your present work without a second thought? And if you did leave, what would you do? (After you took the world cruise, I mean.)

Don't tell me you could just goof off forever, because I don't believe you. I know too many retired people who, after about six months of retirement, become consultants, start new businesses, or do volunteer work. The healthy human soul needs to work and to accomplish.

Go ahead and fantasize freely. Think about what you always wanted to do and forget about your limitations for a few minutes. (Actually, the longer you can forget about your limitations, the more likely you are to accomplish far beyond them.) Keep working to make those fantasies part of your work. For example, even if you decide you're always going to be in an unskilled job, you can still work on a committee to improve conditions in your workplace, or head a scout troop on weekends.

Control

Lack of control leads to fatigue, resentment, and poor performance, all of which add up to stress. When you gain some control over your work, it can seem much less like a job and more like a career. You can never control every aspect of your work; that's not realistic. Many days, even the most glamorous career is nothing but a job.

Even if your job is marked by a high degree of outside control—like supervisors and repetitive procedures—there is some part of it that you can control. If you were in prison or some other impossible situation, how would you keep your sanity? You might make up jokes about it, keep a journal of your experiences, work on an escape plan—or all of the above. Even if these coping strategies seem like desperate measures, they give you some degree of mental control, which ultimately can lead to practical solutions too.

Mastery

This comes from a combination of commitment and control. It means that you want to keep getting better at what you do, and you keep opening up new areas of growth when those around you are bored silly and convinced (incorrectly) that they cannot go further.

It's a mistake to assume that you have reached some stopping point. You may not get any taller or any younger, but your inner self needs to continue to grow, just as it did when you were six; this is the urge toward mastery. If you ignore it, you're heading into a dead end.

Managing Change

It's so easy to get stale. One minute you're comfortable, the next minute you're obsolete.

Change is going on all around you, with or without your consent. So you will be happier—and less likely to stagnate—if you learn to manage it. The human brain loves a routine, so most of the time we ignore, avoid, and even fight change at work.

What's so good about change?

1. Change can keep your brain sharp.
2. Managing change can help you survive instead of becoming obsolete.
3. Change offers opportunities, if you know how to identify them.

Housecleaning Your Brain

When you stick to a routine, you don't learn much; you just repeat the same operations. But when change occurs, your brain wakes up and becomes more alert. During periods of change, you will find ideas flowing as your brain works to solve unexpected problems.

Instead of thinking of change as a nuisance, think of it as a time of growth, opportunity, and fun.

Keep Yourself Current

Whether you're 55 or 25, the minute you say, "I'll never be able to learn this new way of doing things," you brand yourself as an old fuddy-duddy. The people who thrive in times of change are those who leap on new technologies and methods. The rest gather cobwebs—and maybe unemployment checks too.

Sure, that new computerized inventory system is complicated. Sure, the old way seems easier. But the old way was once a new way that seemed impossible to learn. But you did learn it somehow.

There are all types of mentors, so find yourself a technology mentor. Ask for help from the person who knows the most about the new system. You'll learn more quickly from someone who is competent and enthusiastic.

Moments of Opportunity: The New Regime

Let's say you've been pestering your boss for months to move you into a job with some new responsibilities. No luck. Then you get a new boss. What's the first thing you should do? Start building an alliance with the new boss, keeping in mind your goal of getting that job—or maybe even a better opportunity that the new boss has in mind.

Some would argue that when a new boss comes in, the previous boss's employees are goners. As soon as humanly possible, the new boss will try to move in his own trusted people or hire new ones, and the "leftover" employees will be shuffled off to the side. That's often true, but guess who's most likely to get shuffled aside? The worker who makes it clear that she is not willing to change or cooperate with the new regime.

Take the opportunity provided by a new boss and news ways of thinking. Identify yourself to the new boss as a team player, someone who is eager to improve the department and the company. You can win his trust and position yourself well during the changeover. How do you make this happen?

Don't Hang Back

As soon as the new boss comes on board, go ahead and introduce yourself, extend a welcome to the department or the company, and briefly explain what you do. Keep your first encounters chatty and nonthreatening.

Begin with some generalities that signal your willingness to get along: "If there is anything I can do to help you get settled in here. . . ."

If the boss asks, you can identify specific problems and offer solutions: "We've been getting a lot of errors in the production department lately. It might be a good idea to have supervisors leave a short report at the end of each shift, so the supervisor coming on duty will know what to watch out for."

Don't accuse, brown-nose, or inform. The reason you picked a specific problem to mention to the new boss is to demonstrate that you understand how the place works, and that you have the ability to make it work better.

You do not want to identify yourself as a tattletale. If you take the high road, your new boss is more likely to trust you. So you don't need to say, "Production errors are up because the midnight supervisor is spending two hours at lunch." Your boss will find that out soon enough.

When the subject comes up in the conversation—say the boss asks you to talk more about what you do—let the boss know what you want. This is so simple, but most people neglect to do it because they think of it as pushy or egotistical. Maybe it is, but wouldn't you rather eliminate the guesswork for your new boss?

Tell the boss what you want, why you think you can accomplish it, and why it would be good for the company: "I think I'm ready to get into purchasing; I've learned that new inventory control software and I think I can save us some money by making some changes."

Hang in There

It's important to remember that any period of change can be an exhausting, frustrating time, so you have to remember to pace yourself and be patient with yourself, the boss, and co-workers. Expect to make mistakes during transitional times, but resolve to learn from them.

Give things time to shake out, and they will. Sooner than you think, a new routine will develop from any period of apparent chaos. Then you'll have just enough time to recover and regroup before some new change will occur. But this time, you'll be ready for it.

What's So Good About Plateaus?

Sometimes you may feel like you're stagnating, but you're just impatient with the pace of change. Are you feeling like a failure? Not moving ahead at your job as quickly as you planned? Sometimes we're a bit too quick to label ourselves failures for the wrong reasons—for example, you may be simply sitting on a career plateau.

Plateaus are a normal part of everybody's work life. We expend time and effort learning the skills that make us good, and when we master those skills, we have arrived at a plateau. During this period, we are practicing and perfecting what we have learned. Over a lifetime of work, we can expect to reach a number of plateaus. So we ought to know how to recognize them and handle them.

Even the most dedicated workaholic reaches plateaus in her career, although the workaholic may be antsy and uncomfortable at this stage, anxious to move on. For the workaholic, not moving is not succeeding. That's short-sighted and a sure way to burn out at an early age.

Even those of us who aren't overachievers tend to push ourselves too hard, feel guilty about our "lack of progress," and judge ourselves by impossibly high standards. We don't take account of the function of time on our careers. In short, we lose perspective on the overall gains we have made, and concentrate on what we haven't done.

Arriving at a plateau gives you time to breathe after a period of concentrated effort. Remember, change—growth, learning—is stressful. Nothing wrong with taking a breather; you earned it.

The Pleasure Factor

I know, it seems almost un-American just to enjoy what you are doing, even for a short time. Everything around us tells us to strive and keep striving. But you should also keep in mind that there's something invigorating about devoting just a little time to enjoying what you've achieved.

Where Am I Now?

Being on a plateau gives you the chance to ask yourself some tough questions. The most important one is, "Now that I'm here, how do I like it?" In general, periodic reevaluations during plateaus enable you to compare what you're actually doing against your values and your long-term goals. If you neglect that opportunity, you become little more than a rat in a maze.

Burnout in Disguise?

Burnout is always a risk, especially after you've worked so hard to reach a certain level of success in business. The critical difference between plateau and burnout is how you feel. If you hate getting up in the morning, it's probably burnout. The good news is that you can use a plateau period to recover from burnout.

Play around with your job a little. Think about it in upside-down, even silly ways, in an effort to get out of your rut. What if, for instance, you reversed the sequence of tasks in your workday? (You don't have to act on these ideas; their main purpose is to re-vitalize your thinking.)

Time to Move On?

When you start to feel restless again, it's time to give yourself a new challenge, set a new goal. If you stay too long on a plateau, your skills can become flabby and your attitude can deteriorate.

What Is Success?

Deciding whether you've merely arrived at another plateau or actually made it depends on your definition of success. What constitutes success for you? How narrow or broad is your definition of success? Are you "successful" only because you take few risks and therefore seldom fail? The answers depend on your personal values.

If you define success *only* as being better (or better paid) than everyone else in your field, you're going to have to get out there and keep climbing until you achieve your definition of success.

But what if, instead, you define success as doing well enough at your job to feel proud of your work and to make a decent living for yourself? If that's the case, you might already be a success.

Just Plain Failure

If that's what it is, so be it. You tried for something, and you didn't make it. Or you made it, but now you realize it just wasn't the right job for you. The important thing is to remember that a failure is part of the process. People *have* failures, but that does not mean they *are* failures.

That reminds me of one more healing property of a plateau. It gives you time to lick your wounds after a failure. When you begin to feel more resilient, you'll know it's time to start plotting for your next success.

Keep Your Eye on the Next Job

One easy way not to become stagnant at work is to keep reminding yourself that this is not the only job you can do, or the only job you will do, until you retire. So, while you continue to do an excellent job in your present position, you should also be planning for your next job. When you're driving a car, you look ahead a few feet and you also look out to the horizon; that way you're always prepared for change. It's precisely the same with your work.

There are two very good reasons for such thinking. One is defensive and the other is offensive, which in this case does not mean being either unstable or excessively ambitious.

Defense

Your job, your company, and your industry are changing all the time. If profits are plummeting and your market is shrinking, you can expect even more change, more heads rolling, more companies collapsing.

In a world of work that is no longer stable, one of the most dangerous assumptions you can make is that you will always be doing the same job, in the same way, for the same boss, in the same place.

Any one—or all—of those factors could change overnight, and frequently they do. If you haven't started planning *before* something happens, it could take you months to react in your own best interests after the fact. You will have to go through the stages of being stunned and demoralized, losing valuable time, momentum, and morale before you can get on with your career.

Meanwhile, if you allow your skills to stagnate, if you get behind in the technology, if you do not keep expanding your expertise, you can become part of a job pool that is overfilled, or, worse, filled with people more qualified than you.

Offense

If complacency is bad for your career, thinking into the future will keep you ahead of the wave of change. To others, it will seem as if you are moving effortlessly into the better jobs in the successful department or company. In fact, it will be because you worked hard, planned well, and prepared yourself.

What exactly do you need to do—and not do? Here is a review of some dos and don'ts.

DO let your natural curiosity lead you to the center of change. Where is the new equipment being installed? Where is staff being added? Watch. Ask questions.

DON'T count on things to stay the same. Maybe your department has always seemed to be immune to budget and staff cuts. Now the bosses may be under orders to make cuts everywhere.

DO build on a solid foundation. Enlarge the circle of your current expertise to include skills that enhance what you already know.

DON'T think you must make a radical career change. In many cases, that's an impractical step.

DO keep up with new methods. You can learn them from others and from reading trade journals.

DON'T become the old geezer who says, "I've been doing my job this way all these years. Why should I change now?" (You don't have to be old to be an old geezer, just resistant to change.)

DO talk to the people in your company who thrive on and instigate change: the people who switched the company from paper to computers; the techies and the tech junkies. They are loaded with information, usually underappreciated, and often love to talk about what they know.

DON'T say, "I'm just here to do my job and go home." Doing your job should include protecting your future by looking at the whole picture. If you develop tunnel vision about your job, one of these days you won't know what hit you.

DO make it your business to know what's going on, from the desk next to yours right on up to the chairman's office. Listen to office gossip, read newspapers and trade journals. Then you won't be surprised when there's a shakeup.

DON'T be intimidated by change. Change can mean professional growth and excitement for you if you view it as an asset, not a threat.

How Happy Are You at Work?

What is a happy employee? It's someone who feels like a well-regarded, well-trained member of the work team. On the first day of a job, most of us start out with a reservoir of enthusiasm and a desire to do our best. Somewhere along the line, that reservoir starts to drain. That's when stagnation sets in. But before you can refill that reservoir, you need to know what has gone wrong.

Take the following quiz, supplied by the Greater Richmond Partnership, Inc., of Richmond, Virginia, and find out just how happy—or unhappy—you are with your work. The questions below illustrate some of the most important areas of employee satisfaction. Once you can see where you are unhappy, you can take steps to change the situation and avoid stagnation before it creeps up on you.

The Happy Employee Quiz

	Yes	No
1. Do I understand my duties? I can do my best work only if I understand what I am supposed to be doing.	☐	☐
2. Have I received proper training? If I am poorly trained, I am likely to become frustrated and lose my motivation to do good work.	☐	☐
3. Does my company offer refresher courses? Continuing education can keep me involved in my work.	☐	☐
4. Do I have room to grow in my job? A boring, repetitive job with few challenges will soon make me miserable.	☐	☐
5. Can I exercise my own judgment on the job? When my company allows me to use my brain to solve problems, I can develop my initiative and self-esteem.	☐	☐
6. Have I been trained in jobs other than my own? Cross-training gives me a greater sense of accomplishment and a better understanding of the whole work process.	☐	☐
7. Do I have a future with this company? A smart boss explains routes of advancement to me and makes it clear how I can achieve better pay and advancement.	☐	☐
8. Are my working conditions safe and comfortable? Nobody can enjoy work in a dreary, dirty, poorly lit, or poorly maintained workplace.	☐	☐

	Yes	No

9. Is my boss reasonable? If the boss gives me un-   □   □
   reasonable assignments or is inconsistent or unfair to me or other employees, I will respond
   with resentment and carelessness.

10. Does my boss tell me when I've done a good job?   □   □
    A good boss is as free with praise as with criticism.

11. Do I understand my pay and benefits? When I   □   □
    understand how my compensation works, I stand
    a better chance of feeling properly paid for my
    work.

If you answered Yes to eight or more of the above questions, you probably feel happy with your job. Take the quiz again in six months. Remember, things change. You may need to make adjustments.

Also, of course, pay close attention to any questions you answered No. These are your areas of unhappiness and dissatisfaction. You should discuss these matters with your boss and agree on ways to make changes. This quiz has merely identified the weak and strong areas of your working conditions. Now your job is to start talking to each other and solve those problems together.

Here's a question about job happiness from a reader in Port Huron, Michigan:

"If doing what you love means making a whole lot less money than doing another job that you would not enjoy as much, how much money is the enjoyment factor worth?"

And the answer is: Plus or minus $1 million per year. That's exactly how much it means to me. On a good day, it's plus $1 million, and on a rotten day it's minus $1 million. It may mean something less (or more) to you.

If you'll permit me a little workplace Zen, you already know the answer. To help you figure out your answer, let's break this apparently cryptic statement down into some components:

1. How do you know you're in love? Whether it's a person or a job, you just know, that's all. If you have to ask, you may just be one of those mournful souls who doesn't realize it when he has a good thing going. More likely, you probably just aren't really all that much in love with your job.

If you love your job and you know it, you're a rare and lucky dog. Most days, you probably won't miss the money you're not making. If you're also lucky enough to be good at what you do, you'll probably make big money eventually anyway.

2. Compute your lifetime batting average. As I mentioned, the value of job happiness can fluctuate wildly, depending on normal cycles of frustration and satisfaction. If you keep all those variables in mind, you'll be better able to evaluate how you're doing in any given week.

Helpful hint: don't make major career decisions on the strength of either a really good day or a really bad day. Wait and watch.

3. Who are your heroes? Do you envy Donald Trump, or the guy who makes chainsaw sculptures on a farm in Vermont? There are no wrong answers—just right answers for you. If you're having trouble spelling out your own true aspirations, the common threads in the stories of your heroes will indicate your path.

4. You can change your mind. Let's say you actually decide to live out your fantasy and make chainsaw sculptures. Once you start, there will be many surprises that you could not possibly have anticipated. Some of them will be delightful, like the creative freedom and the charms of working with nature.

Then again, you may find yourself getting sick of the gasoline smell and chainsaw noise—and those irregular paychecks. After you've given your new job a decent interval, you're allowed to go back to your old job. You're also allowed to try something completely different.

And even if things don't work out, at least you have now

learned something more about your motivation. Try to draw a useful lesson for next time.

And you now have something no one can ever take away from you: if you've tried something different, even if it didn't work out, you know you're more than just a wage slave. That's a powerful gift.

5. Beware of getting your wish. Sometimes, when people finally get to do what they really love, they suffer a letdown. Some of this can be chalked up to the real-life surprises mentioned above. But it could also be a case of "Is this all there is?" syndrome. If this syndrome hits you, don't panic. See it for what it is, a temporary reaction.

6. Make compromises. Sorry, but you just can't have it all your way. You may find that you must work at a job you hate for six months of the year to buy the freedom of doing the less-profitable work you like for the other six months. It's not perfect, but it's a workable tradeoff. If you can view change as opportunity and if you're willing to make sacrifices for your goal, you'll figure out a method that works for you.

With a family, your compromises will be greater, but you don't have to bury your personal goals. Your decisions will be influenced by your family, but don't lie to yourself. If you start by being honest about what you need, the solutions you reach together will be more effective.

Stagnation is what happens to you when you don't take steps to correct burnout, which then becomes a chronic condition. Stagnation also sets in when you ignore the healthy impulse to grow, and stay still even when you know it's time to move on in your work. Chances are, if you're like most people, you're stagnating right now. Stand up on that career plateau and look around for your next challenge.

Chapter 10

Letting Go of Your Dreams

The Number One Dumb Career Move

You probably already heard the quote from Thomas Alva Edison about genius being "1 percent inspiration and 99 percent perspiration." In this chapter we're going to talk about a third element: aspiration. Along with inspiration and perspiration, you need your aspirations—your dreams—to motivate you.

OK, let's get the excuses out of the way first. Here is what you tell yourself about why you can't accomplish your secret dream:

- You're too busy.
- It's too scary.
- It's too much work.

- It was just a silly idea.
- You'll never make it anyway.

Now that that's over with, let's move on. These excuses (and all their many variations) should sound familiar. They are used by 95 percent of the population, otherwise known as people who don't take chances to make their dreams come true. Are you one of them? Would you like to take your dreams back?

Recently I got a call from a man who wanted help marketing his inventions. He had filed one patent for an invention but he hadn't hit it big yet. He wanted to make enough money from patents so that he could buy a boat. "I want to go fishing every day," he told me.

He was 83 years old.

At first he just seemed pitiful. But then I thought about it. What was the alternative? Saying, "Forget about it. I'll never get that one invention that buys me the boat." And then where would he be? He'd be 83 years old with no dreams and no hopes. Maybe his dream wasn't all that grand. So what? It was his dream and he was working on making it come true.

So, believe it or not, it won't be a tragedy if he doesn't score with his dream of being an inventor. The real tragedy would be if he didn't have any dream at all.

Now, let's make sure you don't turn into a tragedy. What about your dream? One very important thing to remember about dreams is not to limit them. So, as you start to think about your dreams, think big, and then think bigger. Furthermore, you're allowed to dream about something outside your job.

Although this book is about your career, I hope you've figured out by now that your career will be more meaningful to you if it's a part of your whole life. If you can manage it, it's a good goal to connect your job to the rest of your life. Heck, there's a dream for you right there, if you're looking for one.

What I'm trying to say here is that there's a difference between a goal (limited, specific) and a dream (big, complex). When you're putting together your dreams, step back and look for the big picture. That includes such issues as "What do I want to be doing with my life in 5, 10, 20 years?"

Let's start by assuming you are procrastinating on your dream, or having trouble even articulating what it is. What if you had only one year left to live? According to Stephen Levine, a New Mexico therapist who works with dying patients, the top five regrets of dying people are as follows:

- They were sorry they didn't reach their goals or dreams.
- Many would have changed jobs, working less for the money and prestige and more for personal satisfaction and social good.
- Spouses wished they had divorced rather than staying with a mismatched partner.
- Some, especially those between 30 and 50, regretted that they didn't play more.
- Those with money or status realized there was little joy in their lives.

You don't want to end up on your deathbed with a pile of regrets like that, do you? Well then, all you have to do is turn those regrets into wishes and customize them to your own life, and you are ready to get to work on that dream of yours.

Not that it's easy work. Levine wrote the book *One Year to Live: How to Live This Year as if It Were Your Last* (Bell Tower). He says it's hard work. We figured that was the case, but let's get on with it anyhow. Life is short.

I'm very big on New Year's resolutions and those end-of-decade reviews of your life—any opportunity to check in and see how and what you're doing and how you feel about that. I save articles with titles like "30 Things You Should Accomplish Before You're 30" and "40 Things. . . ." You get the idea. You want to keep on top of your dreams, because those years—and decades—roll by so fast.

I also love to hear about people who finally succeed at what they've been working on for years without recognition. Two young men in Massachusetts invented a group of fantasy cartoon characters called Teenage Mutant Ninja Turtles. They became the creators of a very popular toy and television show. Besides making them successful and wealthy, their cartoon opened new career worlds and new dreams: toy manufacturing and marketing, television, animation, and much more.

One day they were geeks drawing cartoon turtles; the next day, they were on top of the world. What happened? Well, nothing really changed. They just kept on working until they achieved recognition, and things started to happen for them.

You probably indulge in your own regular fantasies about quitting and opening a bakery in Boulder, or something else that is completely different from what you're doing now.

One Important Rule

You can make it happen. But you must remember this: don't quit your day job until you've laid the proper groundwork. This may sound too practical while you're still formulating your dream, but before you jump, you need a stable platform from which to leap.

Sometimes we are so afraid that we won't have the courage to make a change because we have waited so long to take a step. Then we force ourselves into an abrupt, dramatic change, as if by doing so we can keep ourselves from turning back. This usually ensures setbacks and disillusionment, because it replaces planning with bravado. It might seem like the right thing to do, just burning all bridges. But you're more likely to succeed if you proceed with your eyes open.

Taking a calculated risk means that you weigh all possible outcomes, good against bad. You consider the effect of the change on your family and on you. You realistically decide how much it will cost you—in money, stress, and all other factors—to make a change in your career, and how much time the transition will take. After you have planned and previsualized every step of the way, then go ahead and quit your job—and savor the feeling.

Are You a Risk Taker?

Maybe you don't change because you don't see yourself as the risk-taking type. First, despite what the pop-psych articles claim, there is no "type." Second, don't think of it as risk—think of it as growth, a much less threatening idea (and a much more healthy one).

Everybody Thinks You're Nuts

Maybe everybody thinks what you want to do is a bad idea and tries to talk you out of it. Well, everybody doesn't have to live with the consequences of your decision, but you do. You are not your friends, and you are not your parents. Listen to people who care about you, but make your own decision.

Research That Dream

One of the things that stops us from changing is fear of the unknown. If you thoroughly research your subject, then it won't be unknown. Talk to people who have done what you want to do. A friend of mine who followed her dream and lived for a year in Paris admitted to me that even the most glamorous city in the world can be dirty, depressing, and lonely. She got through a long winter there, but you could prepare yourself better still. With the kind of real-life knowledge other people can share with you, you can better judge if you still want to leave home for the Left Bank. And if you do it, you'll also prepare yourself for that long, lonely winter.

If you fear failure, concentrate instead on what will happen if you succeed. And if you try and fail, so what? Even if you screw up now, the next time you try something it will be easier, but only if you insist on learning something from each setback and refuse to blame yourself.

Should you try something different if you're happy with what you're doing? Maybe not right this minute, but think back to the last time you were this happy with your job. How long did it last? What changed? Know yourself well enough to know how long it takes you to get restless. Look now for the seeds of discontent. Is your job starting to get easy? Are you starting to feel restless? Always keep your mind open to the next step.

Here's How to Find Those Dreams

Maybe you don't take a chance because you can't imagine what else you'd do.

Think back to when you were in grade school, high school, or maybe college—the times when you thought you could be anything. Some of your fantasies in those days were your best hopes for yourself. Remembering them can remind you of some of your talents that were never realized.

Think forward. Some of us evolve more slowly, and it takes us longer to realize what kind of work makes us feel fulfilled. Maybe you started out wanting a job that provided lots of money and travel. Now what you want is a job that allows you to do something for someone else.

There are many chances you can take that can eventually affect your lifelong dreams because they change you. Master something you're afraid of, or master a bad habit. If you're afraid of the water, learn to swim. Then you can learn to sail, water ski, or scuba dive—or teach children with disabilities to swim. If you lose weight or take a three-month sailing trip, you could end up managing a weight-loss center or writing an article for a sailing magazine.

The chance you take doesn't have to be something that will lead to more money or a promotion. But it should stretch your horizons. After trying something new, make it a practice to check in and see how you're different. Almost as important as trying new things is noticing how they change you.

Most of us ride on a fairly narrow track throughout our careers, rejecting many options. We didn't take dance lessons or go to art school because our parents told us we couldn't make a living at it.

But if you're old enough to pay your own rent, you're old enough to try some of the things you got talked out of way back when. Learn to cook or play golf or piano. These activities will in turn lead you to new friends, new interests, new ways to make a living. It's not a straight path to bigger dreams, but it's a sure one.

The Inspiration File

If your problem is not dreaming big enough, try keeping an inspiration file—a place where you can grow your dream. I keep an inspiration file, and you should do the same. If you have more than one dream, keep several inspiration files. Mine contains a collection of things that keep up my spirits, from the practical to the fantastic: newspaper clippings about people who have made remarkable accomplishments, quotations from great people, even fantasies about what TV shows I want to appear on after I become a famous author.

You can collect words, objects, pictures, whatever inspires you. If you prefer, you can pin your inspirations on a bulletin board, carry them in your wallet, or hey, even sing them to yourself. Just do whatever you need to do to remind yourself of your dream on a daily basis.

Let me give you an example. I hope it will give you insight into how the file can work for you. You may not even understand exactly why you put something into your inspiration file. I have kept one clipping of a column I wrote 11 years ago, and was never sure why—until I looked at it today. It's about a man who had a degree in an obscure subject, geomancy, who later became an author.

Well, duh! I, too, have an obscure degree—philosophy—and I started dreaming about becoming an author soon after interviewing Steven Bennett, a geomancer. (To save you a trip to the dictionary, a geomancer practices the ancient Chinese science of locating buildings in the correct spatial and spiritual alignment.)

I'm telling you this story to illustrate that it sometimes takes a while to articulate what your dream is. However, I do recommend that when you add an item to your inspiration file, you study it and pin down exactly what it is that's inspiring you. Then you might not have to wait 11 years!

Looking again at the Bennett article, it now seems immensely clear what the attraction was: since I was a person who took years to find my focus in life, Bennett's story gave me hope that it could be done.

So an item in your inspiration file may not be about a specific goal or direction. It may, as it was in this case for me, be about the process of getting from where you are now to where you want to be.

This is important: there should be no censor on your inspiration file. That's why I mentioned even singing it to yourself, if that's what does the trick for you. Your inspiration file should be a place where you can dream freely, where one dream can lead to another, where you can go for a shot of courage when you need it—and you will need it.

Let your inspiration file take any form you want. I notice that artists, designers, and other visual people like to have things out where they can see them: sketches, swatches of fabric, even a tree limb, might be tacked to a bulletin board, displayed on a table, or hung from the ceiling. You might prefer to carry a tape recorder or unlined sketch pad. Your inspiration file can take any or all of those forms.

Enjoy it, take good care of it, and feed it frequently, because it is the tangible record of your dreams. It makes them official. I'm a strong believer in "testifying" your dreams, declaring them first to yourself and then to the world.

If you're at the other end of the spectrum, if your dream is big and unwieldy, or if you have tons of dreams and don't know what to do with them all, read the chapter on goal setting one more time (Chapter 4).

But please, work on your dream every day.

Give Your Dream a Name

Here's one important difference between New Year's resolutions and dreams: we often spoil the future by viewing it through the mistakes of the past. That's the trouble with resolutions. Too often they focus on faults instead of possibilities. It's easy to turn the end of the year into a nice little orgy of self-punishment, berating yourself for opportunities missed, fretting that others are moving past you on that ladder whose top is never seen.

Instead, use that time to name your dreams. Dreams are more farsighted than resolutions. Rather than referring to faults that must be overcome, dreams push us out to the limits of our best abilities. Dreams surprise us and delight us.

I've seldom talked to anyone who doesn't have some secret dream to confide. The dreams are paradoxical and touching, and have far more to do with satisfaction than with money or power. A successful business owner wants to write an inspirational book. A reporter wants to start a landscape service. A working mother wants to open a high-quality child care center.

If you can't come up with your own dream right away, it's probably because you haven't allowed yourself time to think about it. Get your mind off your current job and into the realm of pleasant and outrageous fantasy. Dream about doing what you love. What are the things you've always said you wished you could do eight hours a day? (No illegal activities, please.) If it works better for you, you can back into your dream, visualizing the rewards, like the man who wanted to sell an invention so he could afford to fish all the time.

Just don't allow yourself to think, "No, that would never work." Let one idea drift into another. The purpose of the exercise is to get you to think about what you want, not what you think you should want.

What if you're happy just as you are? Having a dream doesn't necessarily imply criticism of your current situation. But it does acknowledge that inevitably you'll outgrow it. A number of variables contribute to making you happy now: you like the team you're on, your boss is crazy about you, you haven't been doing the job long enough to be restless yet.

It's human nature not to think about the future until the present is making you very, very unhappy. That's when you get cornered into making bad decisions. What will you do when the variables begin to shift and you're not as happy as you were? Will you hang on, hoping they'll shift back (they won't), or will you visualize a new plateau to reach?

As long as you're working toward your dream, you'll have that feeling of energy that you always envied in other people. Before, when you were just drifting, things got shuffled aside, piled up, abandoned. Now it will be easier to organize, because you can evaluate every action and set priorities: "If I do this, will it help make my dream happen, or will it only distract me?"

Along the way to your dream, you may make some surprising discoveries that can change your direction. You may have convinced yourself that you were working for prestige or money— and now realize a growing need to do some good for others. When people feel a letdown upon reaching an important milestone, it's sometimes because they realize that getting there did not provide the satisfaction they expected. Be prepared to make adjustments in your dream.

Keep your balance. If working on your dream draws you away from friends and family, you may have the blinders strapped on too tight. A certain amount of obsession is necessary to reach your dream, but it shouldn't deaden you. A dream that isolates you from others can rob you of long-term happiness.

Happy new dreams.

About the Author

Lona O'Connor has been writing about careers for news-papers and magazines since 1981, when her "Work Life" column began in the *Detroit Free Press*. Her column is now published in a number of newspapers across the country.

Born in Buffalo, New York, and raised in Bradenton, Florida, she has been a journalist since age 13, working as a reporter, editor, and photographer. Her freelance work has also appeared in many publications, including *Cosmopolitan, People,* and *Advertising Age*. She now works as a reporter for the *Sun-Sentinel* newspaper in Fort Lauderdale, Florida.

Her husband, Mark, is a newspaper editor. They have one daughter, Nora.

You can contact Lona O'Connor on her web page at www.sun-sentinel.com/money/careers/careers.htm. E-mail: Lona13@AOL .com. Please include your name, address, and phone number.